GCSE AQA

German

There's no need to worry about the GCSE German exams with this CGP Workbook.

It has lots of exam-style questions to test you on reading, writing, listening <u>and</u> speaking, plus grammar practice to check you know your nominative from your accusative.

We've also included lots of online practice in CGP RevisionHub — it has all the audio you need for the speaking and listening questions, plus model answer videos to help you get the most out of your revision. You'll have aced the exams before you know it!

Unlock *CGP RevisionHub*

Just scan a QR code in the book to access the CGP RevisionHub.
Or go to **cgpbooks.co.uk/revise** and enter this code!

2485 3671 0918 5854

By the way, this code only works for one person. If somebody else has used this book before you, they might have already claimed the code.

Exam Practice Workbook

with new *CGP RevisionHub*

Contents

Contents

Published by CGP

Editors:
Lorna Kimmins
Nathan Leach
Ali Palin

With thanks to Margit Grassick, Polly Jackson, Rose Jones and Ben Merritt for the proofreading.
With thanks to Alice Dent for the copyright research.

Acknowledgements:

Audio produced by Voice Talent Online.

AQA material is reproduced by permission of AQA.

*The worked solutions to questions and commentaries on questions and possible answers
in this book have neither been provided by nor approved by AQA.*

ISBN: 978 1 83774 196 0
Printed by Sterling, Kettering.
Clipart from Corel®

How To Use This Book

My parents wanted me to be a doctor or a lawyer when I grew up, but I found my true calling — explaining how books work. Stand back folks and prepare to be wowed...

This book follows the AQA specification

1) The content for AQA GCSE German is divided into **nine topics**.
   Each topic falls under one of **three themes**:

People and lifestyle	Popular culture	Communication and the world around us

2) In this book, there is usually **one** section for each topic. However, some topics have been **split into two sections** to make things more manageable. There's also a section of **mixed practice** at the end of each theme.

3) Section One covers **'General Stuff'**, with content that's useful across the course.

4) There are also three **grammar sections** that cover the grammar you need to know.

You can sit Higher or Foundation tier

1) You can choose to sit the **Higher-tier exams** or the **Foundation-tier exams**. You have to do the **same** tier for all four German exams. Here are the main **differences** between them:

   - In **Foundation tier**, there's **less vocabulary** and **less grammar** to learn and the questions are slightly easier. In this tier, you can earn up to **Grade 5**.
   - In **Higher tier**, you can achieve **Grades 4-9**, but you'll need to learn **more vocab** and **more complex grammar**.
   - Speak to your **teacher** if you're not sure **which tier** you're sitting.

   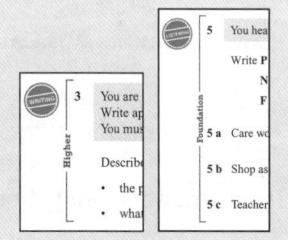

2) In this book, questions that are specific to one of the tiers have been marked up with a **bracket**, like this:

The CGP RevisionHub is full of resources

- You can use the online resources on the CGP RevisionHub **alongside this book** as you're revising.
- The RevisionHub contains all the **audio** you'll need for the **listening questions**, and **speaking tracks** so you can hear the teacher part for all the speaking questions in the book.
- There are printable versions of the **transcripts** and Speaking and Writing **mark schemes** as well.
- It's also got **worked answer videos** for some of the questions, so you can feel more confident about how to answer them.

Scan this QR code to access the CGP RevisionHub, or go to www.cgpbooks.co.uk/haus

Now it's time to get to the good stuff...

No, I'm not talking about a pizza party. It's the heaps of exam practice stuffed into the book, pepperoni'd with lots of helpful videos in the RevisionHub, of course. Argh, I can't stop thinking about pizza...

Numbers, Times and Dates

1   You hear Paul talking about his plans for the year.
Which times and dates does he mention? Complete the table in **English**.

Listening
Track 1

His birthday	Holiday in Switzerland	A wedding
Friday		

[2 marks]

2   Translate the following sentences into **German**.

Example
Answer Video

2 a   April is in Spring.

....

.... *[2 marks]*

2 b   On Tuesdays I go to the park.

....

.... *[2 marks]*

2 c   There are about thirty houses.

....

.... *[2 marks]*

2 d   In the afternoon I should ring my grandad.

....

.... *[2 marks]*

2 e   Yesterday I left school at half past four.

....

.... *[2 marks]*

3 You read these directions on a theatre's website.
Answer the following questions in **English**.

> Von der Stadtmitte aus kann man das Theater in fünfzehn Minuten zu Fuß erreichen. Vom Bahnhof geht man die Hauptstraße entlang*, bis man zum Kino kommt. Nach dem Kino muss man dann die dritte Straße rechts nehmen. Das Theater liegt auf der linken Seite.
>
> Man kann auch mit dem Auto zum Theater fahren. Es gibt einen großen Parkplatz**, der nur ungefähr vierzig Meter vom Theater liegt. Das ist sehr praktisch. Man muss aber zehn Euro pro Stunde für das Parken zahlen.
>
> *entlang = along
> **Parkplatz = car park

3 a How long does the walk from the town centre to the theatre take?

.... *[1 mark]*

3 b Which street do you take after the cinema?

.... *[1 mark]*

3 c How far is the car park from the theatre?

.... *[1 mark]*

3 d How much does parking cost per hour?

.... *[1 mark]*

4 Lara is talking about a concert she is going to.
Listen to what she says and answer the questions in **English**.

Listening Track 2

4 a When is Lara going to a concert?

.... *[1 mark]*

4 b How much are the tickets for the concert?

.... *[1 mark]*

4 c How long did Lara save up to buy her ticket?

.... *[1 mark]*

Higher

Score:

Questions and Being Polite

1 Using your knowledge of grammar, complete the following sentences in **German**.
Choose the correct German word from the three options in the grid.
Write the correct **word** in the space.

1 a .... er nach Italien?

| Reist | Reise | Reisen |

[1 mark]

1 b Ich möchte .... Stück Kuchen.

| ein | einem | einen |

[1 mark]

1 c Dürfen .... die Fenster öffnen?

| er | wir | du |

[1 mark]

2 You will hear 4 short sentences. Listen carefully and, using your knowledge of German sounds, write down in **German** exactly what you hear for each sentence.

You will hear each sentence **three** times: the first time as a full sentence, the second time in short sections and the third time again as a full sentence.

Use your knowledge of German sounds and grammar to make sure that what you have written makes sense. Check carefully that your spelling is accurate.

Listening Track 3

2 a **Sentence 1**

....

.... *[2 marks]*

2 b **Sentence 2**

....

.... *[2 marks]*

2 c **Sentence 3**

....

.... *[2 marks]*

2 d **Sentence 4**

....

.... *[2 marks]*

3 You read this email Julia sent to a restaurant.

> *Guten Morgen,*
>
> *letzte Woche hat meine Schwester mir von Ihrem Restaurant erzählt und ich wollte sofort besuchen. Ich möchte morgen im Restaurant mit meinem Mann essen, aber ich habe ein paar Fragen an Sie.*
>
> *Darf ich meinen Hund zum Restaurant mitbringen? Auch esse ich kein Fleisch und keinen Fisch. Gibt es etwas auf der Speisekarte für mich?*

Answer the following questions in **English**.

3 a How did Julia hear about the restaurant?

.... *[1 mark]*

3 b When does Julia want to eat in the restaurant?

.... *[1 mark]*

3 c What **two** pieces of information does Julia want to know?

1. ....

2. .... *[2 marks]*

4 Translate the following sentences into **German**.

4 a They always thank me warmly.

....

.... *[2 marks]*

4 b What did she need the money for?

....

.... *[2 marks]*

4 c What can we play without bothering him?

....

.... *[2 marks]*

Score:

Opinions

1   You read these reviews of a visit some people made to a botanical garden.

> **Klaas**: Normalerweise gehe ich gern zum Garten, weil ich mich für Pflanzen interessiere. Jedoch war das Wetter schrecklich und ich konnte nichts genießen. Ich habe ein Buch über die Geschichte vom Garten gekauft. Ich werde es zu Hause lesen.
>
> **Tabea**: Zuerst bin ich ins süße Café gegangen und ich habe einen Kaffee gekauft. Ich habe die viele Bäume geliebt und ich will den Garten bald wieder besuchen.
>
> **Nadiem**: Es hat geregnet, sicher, aber es war mir egal. Ich hatte trotzdem eine tolle Erfahrung. Nächstes Mal muss ich das Café besuchen. Ich habe gehört, dass es fantastisch ist.

Match the correct person with each of the following questions.

Write **K** for **Klaas**

   T for **Tabea**

   N for **Nadiem**.

Write the correct letter in each box.

1 a   Who went to the café?

[1 mark]

1 b   Who bought a book?

[1 mark]

1 c   Who didn't mind the weather?

[1 mark]

1 d   Who liked the trees?

[1 mark]

1 e   Who is interested in plants?

[1 mark]

2   You are emailing your Swiss penfriend about books and TV.
Write approximately **90** words in **German**.
You must write something about each bullet point.

Describe:

- which types of books you like to read

- what you thought about the last TV programme you watched

- whether you prefer reading or watching TV, and why.   *[15 marks]*

3 Rory and Priya are making plans for the weekend. Answer the questions in **English**.

Listening Track 4

3 a Why doesn't Rory want to play tennis?

.... *[1 mark]*

3 b What does Priya think of swimming?

.... *[1 mark]*

3 c What did Priya's sister think of the new film?

.... *[1 mark]*

3 d What does Rory say about the previous film?

.... *[1 mark]*

4 Some Austrian teenagers describe their holidays.

> **Elif:** Leider war das Klima nicht das beste. Trotz des schrecklichen Wetters habe ich aber die Museen genossen.

> **Lukas:** Es gab so viele Touristen, dass alle Restaurants und Cafés voll waren. Ich habe es überall schlimm gefunden.

> **Samira:** Die Fahrt zum Hotel war total einfach. Die Stadt, die in der Nähe lag, war auch unglaublich schön.

> **Jan:** Nächstes Jahr würde ich gern wieder ins Hotel gehen, wo ich dieses Jahr gewohnt habe. Es hat mir sehr gut gefallen.

What is the opinion of each teenager about their holiday?

Write **P** for a **positive** opinion

    N for a **negative** opinion

    P + N for a **positive** and **negative** opinion.

Write the correct letter in each box.

Higher

4 a Elif ☐

[1 mark]

4 b Lukas ☐

[1 mark]

4 c Samira ☐

[1 mark]

4 d Jan ☐

[1 mark]

Score: ☐

About Yourself and My Family & Friends

1   You are writing an email to a Swiss exchange student about your life.
Write approximately **90** words in **German**.
You must write something about each bullet point.

Describe:

* where you were born

* who you live with now

* what you're going to do with a family member next week.   *[15 marks]*

2   You will hear 4 short sentences. Listen carefully and, using your knowledge of
German sounds, write down in **German** exactly what you hear for each sentence.

Listening
Track 5

You will hear each sentence **three** times: the first time as a full sentence,
the second time in short sections and the third time again as a full sentence.

Use your knowledge of German sounds and grammar to make sure that what
you have written makes sense. Check carefully that your spelling is accurate.

2 a   Sentence 1

....

....   *[2 marks]*

2 b   Sentence 2

....

....   *[2 marks]*

2 c   Sentence 3

....

....   *[2 marks]*

2 d   Sentence 4

....

....   *[2 marks]*

Higher

3 You are writing an article for young people about family and friends.
Write approximately **150** words in **German**.
You must write something about both bullet points.

Describe:

- the importance of family to you

- a positive experience that you have had with your friends.

[25 marks]

4 You read a newsletter article by Leon about places he has lived. Answer the questions below in **English**.

Vor fünf Jahren wohnte ich mit meinem Vater und meiner Mutter in einer Wohnung in Heidelberg, wo ich geboren bin. Für mich war alles wunderbar, denn ich hatte in der Schule viele Freunde und Heidelberg war hübsch und es gab viel zu tun.

Dann ist meine Oma, die achtzig Jahre alt ist und in Berlin wohnt, sehr krank geworden. Wir mussten deswegen umziehen* und jetzt wohnen wir zusammen in der Hauptstadt.

Am Anfang war ich sehr traurig, dass ich nicht mit meinen Freunden in Heidelberg war, aber das Leben hier in Berlin ist sogar noch besser als in Heidelberg. Meine Familie ist mir auch wichtiger als meine Freunde, und ich kann jeden Tag mit meinen Freunden online sprechen.

*umziehen = to move

4 a Why did Leon like where he used to live? Give **two** details.

1. ....

2. .... *[2 marks]*

4 b Why did his family have to move to where his grandma lives?

.... *[1 mark]*

4 c How does Leon find life in Berlin now?

.... *[1 mark]*

Score:

Describing People and Relationships

1 You see this photo on social media.
What is in this photo?
Write **five** sentences in **German**.

Example
Answer Video

1 a .... *[2 marks]*

1 b .... *[2 marks]*

1 c .... *[2 marks]*

1 d .... *[2 marks]*

1 e .... *[2 marks]*

Foundation

2 You are talking to your German friend. Your teacher
will play the part of your friend and will speak first.

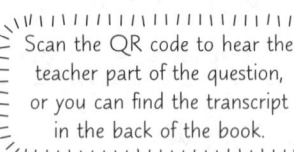
Scan the QR code to hear the
teacher part of the question,
or you can find the transcript
in the back of the book.

Speaking
Track 1

- You should address your friend as *du*.

- When you see this – **?** – you will have to ask a question.

> **In order to score full marks, you must include a verb in your response to each task.**
>
> **1.** Say what your best friend looks like. (Give **one** detail.)
>
> **2.** Give **two** reasons why you like your best friend.
>
> **3.** Say who you get on well with in your family. (Give **one** detail and **one** reason.)
>
> **4.** Say if you would like to get married one day and why / why not.
> (Give **one** opinion and **one** reason.)
>
> **?** **5.** Ask your friend a question about their family.

Higher

[10 marks]

3 Yusuf is talking about his family.
Answer the questions in **English**.

Listening
Track 6

3 a Why does Yusuf often see his aunt?

.... *[1 mark]*

3 b What do Yusuf's friends think about his aunt?

.... *[1 mark]*

3 c Why does Yusuf not get along with his cousin?

.... *[1 mark]*

4 You read this blog post by Lorika, a Swiss celebrity, about her views on relationships.

> Neulich habe ich mich von meinem Partner getrennt. Wahrscheinlich werde ich in der Zukunft heiraten, aber im Moment suche ich nicht nach Liebe, denn ich bin zufrieden mit meinem Leben. Ich habe meinen Traumjob, also möchte ich mich auf meine Arbeit konzentrieren.
>
> Die Ehe ist für mich persönlich wichtig, aber ich verstehe diejenigen, die lieber eine zivile Partnerschaft hätten. Obwohl man nicht unbedingt viel Geld für Hochzeiten ausgeben muss, will ich doch eine große, teure Feier. Außerdem weiß ich, dass Liebe nicht immer einfach ist. Wenn man mit Konflikten auf gesunde Weise umgeht, kann man sogar Probleme in der Beziehung lösen.

Complete these sentences. Write the letter for the correct option in each box.

4 a At the moment, Lorika is...

A	single.
B	in a relationship.
C	about to get married.

[1 mark]

4 b Lorika...

A	is looking for a job.
B	hates her job.
C	loves her job.

[1 mark]

4 c Lorika thinks that...

A	arguments never solve problems.
B	weddings are better than civil partnerships.
C	she will spend a lot of money on her wedding.

[1 mark]

Score:

Find the CGP RevisionHub at cgpbooks.co.uk/haus

Section Two — Identity and Relationships with Others

Food and Healthy & Unhealthy Living

1   When your teacher asks you, read aloud the following text in **German**.

Speaking
Track 2

> Normalerweise esse ich gesund.
>
> Meistens isst meine Familie viel Obst und Gemüse.
>
> Meine Geschwister und ich sind auch sehr aktiv.
>
> Zum Beispiel geht mein Bruder jeden Tag laufen.
>
> Jedoch raucht meine Mutter regelmäßig.

- You will then be asked four questions in **German** that relate to the topic of **Healthy living and lifestyle**.

- In order to score the highest marks, **answer all four questions as fully as you can**.

[15 marks]

2   Using your knowledge of grammar, complete the following sentences in **German**. Choose the correct German word from the three options in the grid. Write the correct **word** in the space.

2 a   Ich trinke .... Alkohol.

keinem	keinen	kein

[1 mark]

2 b   Mein Freund .... jedes Wochenende Sport.

treiben	treibe	treibt

[1 mark]

3   Three German teenagers are talking about keeping healthy. Choose what each teenager mentions and write the correct letter in each box.

Listening
Track 7

A	going to the gym
B	riding a bicycle
C	swimming
D	eating fruit
E	avoiding fast food

3 a   Elif   [　]

[1 mark]

3 b   Julian   [　]

[1 mark]

3 c   Sofie   [　]

[1 mark]

4 You are writing an article for your school magazine about healthy living.
Write approximately **150** words in **German**.
You must write something about both bullet points.

Describe:

• the different factors that contribute to a healthy lifestyle

• what exercise you will do next month. *[25 marks]*

5 You read two posts on a forum about food and people's eating habits.

Alina

Ich versuche immer, gesund zu essen. Mein ganzes Leben lang bin ich Vegetarierin gewesen. Ich finde das gesünder, als viel Fleisch zu essen. Für mich kann das Abendessen eine wichtige soziale Aktivität sein. Ich esse oft mit meinen Freundinnen in der Stadt, was immer schön ist.

Berndt

Ich würde gern gesund essen, aber leider habe ich oft nicht genug Zeit. Ich arbeite viele Stunden und danach habe ich keine Lust mehr, etwas zu kochen. Meiner Meinung nach macht es mehr Spaß, wenn man mit anderen isst. Dann kann man sich mit Menschen unterhalten und etwas zusammen genießen. Es gibt nichts, was ich nicht probieren würde.

Who do the following statements refer to?

Write **A** for **Alina**

B for **Berndt**

A + B for **Alina** and **Berndt**.

Write the correct letter in each box.

5 a Who is too busy to eat healthily?

[1 mark]

5 b Who does not eat meat?

[1 mark]

5 c Who likes to eat with other people?

[1 mark]

Score:

Illnesses and Treatments

1 Your friend Katharina sends you a text message about how she is feeling unwell. Answer the questions below in **English**.

> Hallo. Ich fühle mich heute nicht so gut. Ich habe Kopfschmerzen und Rückenschmerzen. Ich habe mehr geschlafen und viel Wasser getrunken, aber die Schmerzen haben sich noch nicht verbessert. Im Moment kocht mir meine Mutter **Eintopf**, der mir hoffentlich hilft.

1 a Which **two** body parts does Katharina say are hurting?

1. ....

2. .... *[2 marks]*

1 b What has Katharina done to try and get better? Give **two** details.

1. ....

2. .... *[2 marks]*

1 c Read the last sentence again. What would you do with **Eintopf**?

Write the correct letter in the box.

A	bathe in it
B	apply it to skin
C	eat it

[1 mark]

2 You are writing an email to your friend about health concerns. Write approximately **90** words in **German**. You must write something about each bullet point.

Describe:

- a time you went to the doctor's in the past

- what you can do to prevent health problems

- what you will do the next time you feel unwell. *[15 marks]*

Listening
Track 8

3 Herr Hoffmann is talking to his doctor about his health concerns.
Listen to their conversation and answer the questions below in **English**.

3 a What is wrong with Herr Hoffmann?

.... *[1 mark]*

3 b What caused this?

.... *[1 mark]*

3 c What does the doctor say she can do today?

.... *[1 mark]*

Higher

3 d What does the doctor recommend to Herr Hoffmann?

.... *[1 mark]*

3 e What does the doctor give to Herr Hoffmann?

.... *[1 mark]*

Speaking
Track 3

4 Spend a few minutes looking at the two photos.
Make notes on them to use during the test.

Your teacher will ask you to talk about the content of the photos.
You should talk for approximately **one and a half minutes**.
You must say at least one thing about each photo.

After you have spoken about the content of the photos,
your teacher will then ask you questions related to
any of the topics within the theme of **People and lifestyle**.

Higher

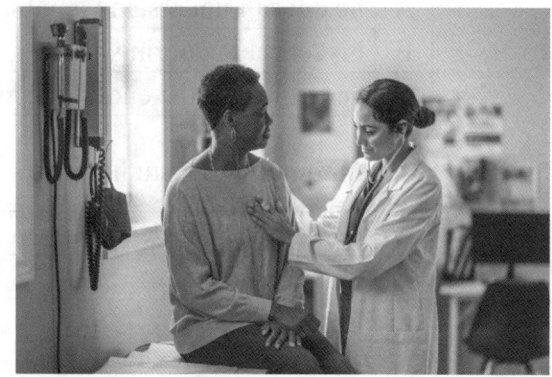

[25 marks]

Score:

School Subjects and School Life

1   When your teacher asks you, read aloud the following text in **German**.

> Täglich fahre ich mit dem Bus zur Schule.
>
> Montags habe ich zuerst Chemie.
>
> Die Stunden sind toll, weil ich meine Lehrer mag.
>
> Aber die Hausaufgaben sind für mich ziemlich schwer.
>
> In der Pause esse ich mein Mittagessen in der Kantine.

- You will then be asked four questions in **German** that relate to the topic of **Education**.

- In order to score the highest marks, **answer all four questions as fully as you can**.

[15 marks]

Foundation (side label)

2   Read Joel's blog post about his school, then complete the sentences below. Write the correct letters in the boxes.

> *Ich finde Mathe blöd, weil der Lehrer langweilig ist. Ich verstehe alles, aber ich warte immer auf das Ende von der Stunde. Dagegen liebe ich Sprachen. Früher habe ich Französisch und Spanisch in der Schule gelernt, aber jetzt lerne ich nur Englisch. Englisch finde ich einfach, weil ich viele englische Videos im Internet sehe.*
>
> *Täglich haben wir um zwölf Uhr eine Pause. Obwohl meine Freunde oft die Pause in der Kantine verbringen, spiele ich lieber auf dem Basketballfeld.*

2 a   Joel doesn't like maths because...

A	he doesn't understand anything.
B	his teacher is boring.
C	he is tired by the end of the lesson.

[1 mark]

2 b   At the moment, Joel studies...

A	French.
B	Spanish.
C	English.

[1 mark]

2 c   At break, Joel often...

A	plays sport.
B	watches videos.
C	reads his book.

[1 mark]

3 You are writing to your German penfriend about your school.
Write approximately **90** words in **German**.
You must write something about each bullet point.

Describe:

• what your favourite subject is and why

• how you got to school last week

• what you will do in PE next week. *[15 marks]*

4 Samira sends you a voice note about her school routine.
Answer the questions in **English**.

Listening
Track 9

4 a What time does Samira's school day start?

.... *[1 mark]*

4 b How does Samira normally travel to school?

.... *[1 mark]*

4 c Which subject does Samira have first?

.... *[1 mark]*

Higher

4 d What did Samira like about going to the canteen at break time?

.... *[1 mark]*

4 e Where does the course that Samira does take place?

.... *[1 mark]*

Score:

Section Four — Education

School Pressures and Difficulties

 1 Four Swiss students are talking about the pressures of school life.

Leni

Meine Lehrer
unterstützen mich.

Gülru

Manchmal gibt
es Mobbing.

Felix

Es gibt viele
Klassenarbeiten.

Bruno

Bald bekomme
ich mein Zeugnis.

What does each student mention?

Write the correct letter in each box.

A	bullying
B	grades
C	school report
D	support
E	rules
F	school tests

1 a Leni ☐

[1 mark]

1 b Gülru ☐

[1 mark]

1 c Felix ☐

[1 mark]

1 d Bruno ☐

[1 mark]

 2 You are writing an article about the pressures at school.
Write approximately **90** words in **German**.
You must write something about each bullet point.

Foundation
Answer Video

Higher
Answer Video

Describe:

• the rules at your school

• what you needed support with in school last year

• how you will deal with difficulties at school next year.　　*[15 marks]*

Section Four — Education

3 You are talking to your German friend. Your teacher will play the part of your friend and will speak first.

Speaking
Track 5

- You should address your friend as *du*.

- When you see this – **?** – you will have to ask a question.

In order to score full marks, you must include a verb in your response to each task.

1. Say what you wear at school. (Give **one** detail.)

2. Say how often you have school tests. (Give **one** detail.)

3. Describe a problem in your school. (Give **one** detail.)

4. Give **one** opinion on exams.

? 5. Ask your friend a question about pressures at school.

[10 marks]

Foundation

---

4 Four friends are talking about what they experience at school.

Listening
Track 10

Write **P** if the experience happened in the **past**

    N if the experience is happening **now**

    F if the experience will happen in the **future**.

Higher

4 a Yuki — classes   ☐

[1 mark]

4 b Mika — exams   ☐

[1 mark]

4 c Hanna — teacher support   ☐

[1 mark]

4 d Jonas — exchange   ☐

[1 mark]

Score:

Education Post-16 and Career Choices

 1 You will hear 2 short sentences. Listen carefully and, using your knowledge of German sounds, write down in **German** exactly what you hear for each sentence.

Listening
Track 11

You will hear each sentence **three** times: the first time as a full sentence, the second time in short sections and the third time again as a full sentence.

Use your knowledge of German sounds and grammar to make sure that what you have written makes sense. Check carefully that your spelling is accurate.

1 a   Sentence 1

....

....   *[2 marks]*

1 b   Sentence 2 *(Higher)*

....

....   *[2 marks]*

 2 You are writing an email to your Austrian friend about your education and future plans. Write approximately **90** words in **German**. You must write something about each bullet point.

Describe:

*   what you're studying at the moment

*   what job you wanted to do when you were younger

*   what job you plan to do in the future.   *[15 marks]*

 **3** You hear some people talking about jobs. Which job does each person want to do? What is **one** quality needed for each job?

Listening
Track 12

Complete the table in **English**.

	Job	Quality
Tove		
Hans		

[4 marks]

Speaking
Track 6

4   You are talking to your Swiss friend. Your teacher
will play the part of your friend and will speak first.

- You should address your friend as *du*.

- When you see this – **?** – you will have to ask a question.

In order to score full marks, you must include a verb in your response to each task.

1. Describe your dream job. (Give **two** details.)

2. Say **two** things you will do after your exams.

3. Give **one** opinion on apprenticeships.

4. Say if you would like to go to university. (Give **one** opinion and **one** reason.)

? 5. Ask your friend a question about their career plans.

[10 marks]

Higher

5   You read this blog post that Sascha has written about his future studies.

---

*Im Moment mache ich das Abitur in der Schule. Meine Lieblingsfächer
sind Mathe, Chemie und Geschichte. Nächstes Jahr muss ich meine
Prüfungen machen. Ich hoffe, dass ich sie bestehen werde.*

*Letzten Sommer habe ich eine Sommerschule in Frankreich besucht,
und danach habe ich ein Angebot bekommen, Chemie an der
Universität zu studieren. Ich bin nicht sicher, ob ich dafür bereit
bin. Meine Eltern haben mir deshalb empfohlen, ein Jahr zu warten.
Inzwischen werde ich einen Teilzeitjob suchen, um Geld zu verdienen.*

What does the blog post say about the following events?

Write **P** for something that happened **in the past**

N for something that is happening **now**

F for something that will happen **in the future**.

Write the correct letter in each box.

Higher

5 a   Doing A levels

[1 mark]

5 b   Summer school in France

[1 mark]

5 c   Passing exams

[1 mark]

5 d   Finding a job

[1 mark]

Score:

Mixed Practice — Foundation

1   Some Austrian teenagers are talking about their family.

> **Schmuel:** *Meine Tante wohnt in meiner Nähe.*
>
> **Lisa:** *Jede Woche helfe ich meinem Opa beim Einkaufen.*
>
> **Emilia:** *Ich komme mit meiner Schwester aus.*

Which family member does each person mention? Write the correct letter in the box.

1 a   Schmuel   ☐

1 b   Lisa   ☐

1 c   Emilia   ☐

A	father
B	sister
C	cousin
D	grandfather
E	aunt

[1 mark]

[1 mark]

[1 mark]

2   Translate the following sentences into **German**.

2 a   My stepbrother is bisexual.

....

....   *[2 marks]*

2 b   My family eats fast food now and then.

....

....   *[2 marks]*

2 c   Tomorrow I will go to the doctor.

....

....   *[2 marks]*

2 d   Last year my teachers were very helpful.

....

....   *[2 marks]*

3 Angela phones you to talk about her school timetable.

Listening Track 13

Write the correct number of the subject she mentions.
Write the correct letter for the time it starts.

Answer both parts of question 3.

	Subject
1	Spanish
2	Geography
3	Cookery
4	Art

	Time
A	9.00 am
B	11.15 am
C	2.30 pm

3 a

Subject ☐

Time ☐

[2 marks]

3 b

Subject ☐

Time ☐

[2 marks]

4 Spend a few minutes looking at the two photos.
Make notes on them to use during the test.

Speaking Track 7

Your teacher will ask you to talk about the content of the photos.
You should talk for approximately **one minute**.
You must say at least one thing about each photo.

After you have spoken about the content of the photos,
your teacher will then ask you questions related to **any** of the topics
within the theme of **People and lifestyle**.

 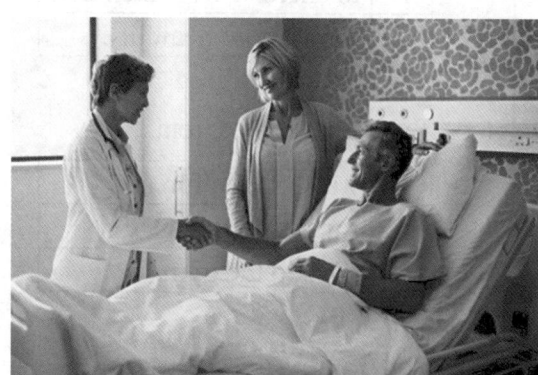

[25 marks]

5 You hear Tobias talking about his work life.

Write **P** if he did the job in the **past**

N if he is doing the job **now**

F if he will do the job in the **future**.

5 a Care worker ☐   *[1 mark]*

5 b Shop assistant ☐   *[1 mark]*

5 c Teacher ☐   *[1 mark]*

Foundation

READING

6 You receive this email from Greta talking about a recent health problem.

> Vor zwei Monaten war ich immer müde und ich hatte wirklich keine Energie. Ich bin zum Arzt gegangen und er hat mir drei Dinge empfohlen: ich muss mehr schlafen, gesünder essen und mich oft bewegen. Nach dem Besuch zum Arzt habe ich einige Sachen in meinem Leben verändert. Ich gehe jetzt um 10 Uhr ins Bett und ich esse mehr Obst und Gemüse. Auch spaziere ich jedes Wochenende mit meinen Freunden im Wald.

Complete these sentences. Write the letter for the correct option in each box.

6 a Two months ago, Greta was always...

A	tired.
B	anxious.
C	sad.

☐   *[1 mark]*

6 b One of her doctor's recommendations was...

A	to go to sleep at 10 pm.
B	to exercise less intensely.
C	to eat more healthily.

☐   *[1 mark]*

6 c Every weekend, Greta...

A	walks in the forest.
B	runs in the park.
C	goes to the gym.

☐   *[1 mark]*

Foundation

Score: ☐

Mixed Practice — Both Tiers

 1 Translate the following sentences into **English**.

Foundation

1 a Montags gehe ich ins Fitness-Studio.

....

.... *[2 marks]*

1 b Die Schülerin fragt nach den Hausaufgaben.

....

.... *[2 marks]*

1 c Ich mag meine Schwester, aber mein Cousin ist gemein.

....

.... *[2 marks]*

1 d Früher wollte er wirklich als Betreuer arbeiten.

....

.... *[2 marks]*

Higher

1 e Meine Eltern haben sich vor fünf Jahren getrennt.

....

.... *[2 marks]*

 2 You are writing to your Swiss penfriend about your friends.
Write approximately **90** words in **German**.
You must write something about each bullet point.

Describe:

• what makes a good friend

• something you did with a friend last week

• what one of your friends will do after leaving school. *[15 marks]*

3 You read this blog post by Romy about relationships. Answer the questions below in **English**.

> *In der Zukunft möchte ich jemanden heiraten, der geduldig, ehrlich und witzig ist. Für mich ist das Aussehen nicht so wichtig, jedoch mag ich keine Gesichtshaare. Ein **Schnurrbart**, zum Beispiel, ist nichts für mich.*
>
> *Aber im Moment will ich keine Beziehung haben, denn ich habe keine Zeit in meinem Leben dafür. Ich möchte viel Zeit mit meinem Partner verbringen, wenn ich einen habe. Mein Bruder hat eine Partnerin und sie ist ziemlich nett. Ich finde es aber traurig, dass sie seine Interessen nicht unterstützt.*

3 a Give **two** personality traits that Romy would like her partner to have.

1. ....

2. .... *[2 marks]*

3 b Why is Romy not looking for a partner at the moment?

.... *[1 mark]*

3 c What does she find sad about her brother's relationship?

.... *[1 mark]*

3 d Read the final sentence of the first paragraph again. What is a **Schnurrbart**?

Write the correct letter in the box.

A	a moustache
B	a piercing
C	a birth mark

[1 mark]

4 A German pupil is talking about her school subjects.
Write the correct letters in the boxes to complete the sentences.
Answer both parts of question 4.

Listening
Track 15

4 a The pupils have PE...

A	at the end of the week.
B	once a week.
C	twice a week.

[1 mark]

4 b The girl who was interviewed...

A	prefers foreign languages.
B	finds maths difficult.
C	likes maths best of all.

[1 mark]

5 Translate the following sentences into **German**.

5 a My father would like to cook today.

....

.... *[2 marks]*

5 b The woman often worries about her health.

....

.... *[2 marks]*

5 c On Sunday we ate ice cream together.

....

.... *[2 marks]*

5 d It is my friend's aim to work in a factory.

....

.... *[2 marks]*

Higher

Score:

Mixed Practice — Higher

Higher

1 You are writing a post for your blog about studying and career aspirations.
Write approximately **150** words in **German**.
You must write something about both bullet points.

Describe:

• the pros **and** cons of studying at university

• what job you would like to do when you're older. *[25 marks]*

2 Translate the following sentences into **English**.

2 a Sie bereitet sich gerade auf das Vorstellungsgespräch vor.

....

.... *[2 marks]*

2 b Ich trinke keinen Kaffee am Abend, um schneller einzuschlafen.

....

.... *[2 marks]*

Higher

2 c Letzten Monat hat er für seine Gesundheit Alkohol aufgegeben.

....

.... *[2 marks]*

2 d Wenn ich älter bin, werde ich viele Tätowierungen haben.

....

.... *[2 marks]*

2 e Als Kind habe ich kaum Sport getrieben, da es anstrengend war.

....

.... *[2 marks]*

3   You read this newsletter article about a new local gymnastics club.

Wollten Sie schon immer mal eine neue Sportart zu einem niedrigen Preis ausprobieren? Vielleicht ist Turnen* für Sie. Wir gründen einen neuen Turnverein im Sportzentrum — die erste Stunde wird nächste Woche am Freitagabend stattfinden. Wir öffnen unsere Türen sowohl für Anfänger als auch für diejenigen, die ihr ganzes Leben lang geturnt haben.

Außerdem werden wir Krafttrainingsstunden organisieren, wenn sich genug Leute dafür interessieren. Das Krafttraining wäre nicht so strikt wie die anderen Stunden, und wir werden in einigen Wochen weitere Informationen mitteilen.

Wir glauben, dass Turnen viel mehr als nur ein Vorteil für die Gesundheit ist. Wenn man eine schwierige Turnbewegung schafft, lernt man, wie man Probleme lösen kann, ohne zuerst aufzugeben. Dadurch lernt man, wie man unter Druck ruhig bleibt, was besonders bei Klassenarbeiten hilfreich sein kann.

Schüler in der Oberstufe haben die Gelegenheit, eine Ausbildung zum Trainer zu machen. Sie würden den Sechzehnjährigen in den Stunden helfen, während sie zur gleichen Zeit Erfahrung für künftige Jobs bekommen.

*Turnen = gymnastics

Complete these sentences. Write the letter for the correct option in each box.

3 a   The gymnastics classes...

A	have not started yet.
B	are only for beginners.
C	cost quite a lot.

[1 mark]

3 b   Strength training classes...

A	are compulsory for some people.
B	happen every week.
C	are more relaxed.

[1 mark]

3 c   According to the article, gymnastics could help you...

A	solve all your problems.
B	make friends for life.
C	perform better in exams.

[1 mark]

3 d   People can start training to be a coach...

A	when they turn sixteen.
B	while they are in sixth form.
C	when they have left school.

[1 mark]

4 You hear Bastian talking to a friend about his relationship. Complete the sentences in **English**.

Listening Track 16

4 a Bastian thinks his relationship with his boyfriend is close because...

.... *[1 mark]*

4 b However, he doesn't like that...

.... *[1 mark]*

4 c Parveen suggests that Bastian...

.... *[1 mark]*

4 d For Parveen, the most important thing in a relationship is that...

.... *[1 mark]*

5 Translate the following sentences into **German**.

5 a This dish is unbelievably tasty.

....

.... *[2 marks]*

5 b Yesterday they promised to be friendlier.

....

.... *[2 marks]*

5 c I got to know an Austrian woman at the wedding.

....

.... *[2 marks]*

5 d Although he studies a lot, he had to repeat a school year.

....

.... *[2 marks]*

5 e I will do an apprenticeship instead of studying at university.

....

.... *[2 marks]*

6 Chibuike is talking about jobs.
What does he say about himself?

Listening Track 17

Write **A** if only statement **A** is correct

B if only statement **B** is correct

A + B if both statements **A** and **B** are correct.

6 a As a child, Chibuike...

A	was good at science.
B	wanted to become a lawyer.

[1 mark]

6 b In a job, Chibuike is looking for...

A	a good work culture.
B	a high salary.

[1 mark]

7 When your teacher asks you, read aloud the following text in **German**.

Speaking Track 8

> Ich mache sehr viel, um in Form zu bleiben.
>
> Ziemlich häufig bewege ich mich in der Turnhalle.
>
> Jedoch sind andere Faktoren für die Gesundheit auch wichtig.
>
> Zum Beispiel esse ich eine gesunde Ernährung mit viel Gemüse.
>
> Außerdem schlafe ich mindestens acht Stunden pro Nacht.
>
> Dadurch fühle ich mich insgesamt wohl.

- You will then be asked four questions in **German** that relate to the topic of **Healthy living and lifestyle**.

- In order to score the highest marks, **answer all four questions as fully as you can**.

[15 marks]

Score:

Cinema, TV and Music

1 Spend a few minutes looking at the two photos. Make notes on them to use during the test.

Your teacher will ask you to talk about the content of the photos. You should talk for approximately **one minute**. **You must say at least one thing about each photo**.

After you have spoken about the content of the photos, your teacher will then ask you questions related to **any** of the topics within the theme of **Popular culture**.

Scan the QR code to hear the teacher part of the question, or you can find the transcript in the back of the book.

Foundation

[25 marks]

2 You hear two people talking about films they saw.

Listening Track 18

A	the plot
B	the soundtrack
C	themes
D	actors
E	the location
F	the director

Which **two** things does each person mention?

Write the correct letters in the boxes.

Higher

2 a Tomoki   ☐ ☐

[2 marks]

2 b Charlotte   ☐ ☐

[2 marks]

3 Your Austrian friend sends you an email asking about TV and film.
Write them a reply.
Write approximately **90** words in **German**.
You must write something about each bullet point.

Describe:

- which genres of film and TV you enjoy

- a TV programme you saw recently

- a film you will watch when you go to the cinema.

[15 marks]

4 You read two interviews about the role of music in teenagers' lives.

Higher

Zeynep: Meistens höre ich Lieder, die ich streame, aber manchmal höre ich auch Radio. Rock und Popmusik gefallen mir am besten. Ich würde gern in meinem Leben ein Konzert besuchen, aber ich habe es noch nicht geschafft, denn die Karten sind immer unglaublich teuer. Ich möchte auch ein Instrument lernen, aber ich denke, dass ich nicht musikalisch genug bin.

Moritz: Seit vielen Jahren ist mir Musik sehr wichtig. Als Kind spielte ich mehrere Instrumente, aber im Moment spiele ich nur zwei. Meine Freunde hören am liebsten Pop und Rock, allerdings glaube ich, dass diese Arten von Musik schrecklich klingen. Ich höre lieber Jazz. Ich bin noch nie zu einem Konzert gegangen, aber meine Mutter hat uns Karten für ein Jazzkonzert gekauft, das nächstes Wochenende stattfindet.

Who do the following statements refer to?

Write **Z** for **Zeynep**

M for **Moritz**

Z + M for **Zeynep** and **Moritz**.

4 a Who likes listening to rock music?

[1 mark]

4 b Who has not been to a concert?

[1 mark]

4 c Who plays a musical instrument?

[1 mark]

Score:

Sport, Going Out and Other Hobbies

Example
Answer Video

1 Some young people from Switzerland describe their reading habits.

> **Georg:** Lesen mag ich gar nicht. Ich spiele lieber Fußball und ich habe zweimal pro Woche Training.
>
> **Nasim:** Meine Geschwister lieben Sport, aber ich lese immer. Ich interessiere mich mehr für Zeitungen als Romane und normalerweise lese ich sie jeden Morgen im Bett.
>
> **Bianka:** Wenn ich ausgehe, nehme ich immer einen Roman mit. Jeden Abend lese ich im Bett, weil ich es entspannend finde. Danach schlafe ich immer besser.

Match the correct person with each of the following questions.

Write **G** for **Georg**

    N for **Nasim**

    B for **Bianka**.

Write the correct letter in each box.

1 a Who takes a book everywhere they go?   ☐   *[1 mark]*

1 b Who prefers to read newspapers?   ☐   *[1 mark]*

1 c Who likes to read before sleeping?   ☐   *[1 mark]*

1 d Who likes sport more than reading?   ☐   *[1 mark]*

2 Your German friend writes you an email asking how you spend your free time.
Write them a reply.
Write approximately **50** words in **German**.
You must write something about each bullet point.

Mention:

- sport

- shopping

- reading

- parties

- another free-time activity.   *[10 marks]*

3 Kim is talking about a restaurant he went to.
Answer the questions in **English**.

Listening
Track 19

3 a When did Kim go to the restaurant?

.... *[1 mark]*

3 b How did Kim travel to the restaurant?

.... *[1 mark]*

3 c Why does Kim say the menu is great?

.... *[1 mark]*

3 d What did Kim find annoying?

.... *[1 mark]*

4 Translate the following sentences into **English**.

4 a Ich besuche das Museum, denn ich finde Geschichte interessant.

....

.... *[2 marks]*

4 b Sie läuft schneller als die andere Spielerinnen in der Mannschaft.

....

.... *[2 marks]*

4 c Vor drei Jahren hat er einen Tenniswettbewerb gewonnen.

....

.... *[2 marks]*

5 You are writing a blog post about free-time activities.
Write approximately **150** words in **German**.
You must write something about both bullet points.

Higher

Describe:

• the benefits of doing free-time activities

• which activities you would like to try. *[25 marks]*

Score:

Customs, Festivals and Celebrations

1   You hear Hanna talking about her aunt's wedding.
Choose the correct answer and write the letter in each box.

Listening
Track 20

1 a Hanna's aunt's wedding took place...

A	in spring.
B	on her aunt's birthday.
C	around New Year's Eve.

[1 mark]

1 b Hanna says that...

A	the wedding was a small celebration.
B	her aunt invited lots of friends.
C	there was a tasty meal.

[1 mark]

1 c At the end of the night, Hanna...

A	gave the couple a present.
B	congratulated the couple.
C	danced.

[1 mark]

2   When your teacher asks you, read aloud the following text in **German**.

Speaking
Track 10

> Letztes Jahr habe ich den Karneval toll gefunden, weil die Stimmung schön war.
>
> Normalerweise verbringen wir Ostersonntag bei meinen Großeltern.
>
> In meiner Familie haben wir immer viel Freude am Feiern.
>
> Letztes Weihnachten hat meine Familie mir eine Theaterkarte geschenkt.
>
> Ich glaube, dass die Familie bei Festen das Wichtigste ist.
>
> Ich liebe deshalb Silvester, weil wir das Feuerwerk anschauen.

Higher

- You will then be asked four questions in **German** that relate to the topic of **Customs, festivals and celebrations**.

- In order to score the highest marks, **answer all four questions as fully as you can**.

[15 marks]

3 You are writing about festivals that you celebrate.
Write approximately **90** words in **German**.
You must write something about each bullet point.

Describe:

- what festivals you celebrate

- how you celebrated a festival last year

- a festival you are looking forward to and why.

[15 marks]

4 You read this extract from an article about Carnival.

> In der Schweiz, in Österreich und Deutschland findet Karneval ungefähr sieben Wochen vor Ostern statt. Man feiert Karneval in den verschiedenen Regionen ganz anders, jedoch gibt es viele ähnliche Aspekte. Zum Beispiel gibt es überall Straßenfeste, die mehrere Tage dauern.
>
> Die Ereignisse in Köln sind die bekanntesten in Deutschland. Viele Leute gehen auf die Straßen, um an einem großen Umzug* teilzunehmen. Die Teilnehmer der Parade tragen bunte Kostüme** und Masken. Dazu spielen sie Musik. Bei diesen Umzügen kann man auch traditionelle deutsche Gerichte kaufen.
>
> *Umzug = procession
> **Kostüme = costumes

Higher

4 a When does Carnival take place?

.... *[1 mark]*

4 b Where are the most famous German Carnival events held?

.... *[1 mark]*

4 c What do the participants of the processions do? Give **two** details.

1. ....

2. .... *[2 marks]*

Score:

Favourite Celebrities and Celebrity Life

1 You are talking to your Austrian friend. Your teacher will play the part of your friend and will speak first.

Example
Answer Video

Speaking
Track 11

- You should address your friend as *du*.

- When you see this – ? – you will have to ask a question.

Foundation

> **In order to score full marks, you must include a verb in your response to each task.**
>
> **1.** Say what your favourite celebrity does. (Give **one** detail.)
>
> **2.** Say what your favourite celebrity looks like. (Give **one** detail.)
>
> **3.** Say **one** thing that you like about your favourite celebrity.
>
> **4.** Give **one** opinion about celebrity life.
>
> **? 5.** Ask your friend a question about their favourite celebrity.

[10 marks]

2 You read an extract from the autobiography of a famous actor, Felix Franz.

> Ich bin froh, dass ich so bekannt bin. Die Vorteile davon sind klar: ich habe ein bequemes Leben und ich kann meine Arbeit mit dem Publikum teilen. Aber berühmt sein ist nicht immer einfach. Für mich ist es ärgerlich, wenn Journalisten mir folgen. Viele Stars wollen auch wirklich erfolgreich sein. Meiner Meinung nach sind der Erfolg und die Preise nicht so wichtig. Es ist mir viel wichtiger, dass ich meine Fans glücklich mache.

Answer the following questions in **English**.

2 a According to Felix, what is one benefit of being famous? Give **one** example.

.... *[1 mark]*

2 b What does Felix find annoying about being famous?

.... *[1 mark]*

2 c What is more important to Felix than success?

.... *[1 mark]*

3 You will hear 4 short sentences. Listen carefully and, using your knowledge of German sounds, write down in **German** exactly what you hear for each sentence.

Listening
Track 21

You will hear each sentence **three** times: the first time as a full sentence, the second time in short sections and the third time again as a full sentence.

Use your knowledge of German sounds and grammar to make sure that what you have written makes sense. Check carefully that your spelling is accurate.

3 a   Sentence 1

Foundation

....

.... *[2 marks]*

3 b   Sentence 2

....

.... *[2 marks]*

3 c   Sentence 3

....

.... *[2 marks]*

3 d   Sentence 4

Higher

....

.... *[2 marks]*

4 You are writing an article about celebrity culture for a German magazine.
Write approximately **150** words in **German**.
You must write something about both bullet points.

Higher

Describe:

• the positive **and** negative aspects of being a celebrity

• which celebrity you would most like to meet. *[25 marks]*

Score:

Mixed Practice — Foundation

1   When your teacher asks you, read aloud the following text in **German**.

Speaking
Track 12

> In meiner Freizeit gehe ich oft ins Kino.
>
> Mein Lieblingsfilm ist eine sehr lustige Komödie.
>
> Ein bekannter Schauspieler spielt die Hauptrolle.
>
> Früher war er ein erfolgreicher Sänger.
>
> Ich habe alle seine Lieder gehört.

- You will then be asked four questions in **German** that relate to the topic of **Free-time activities**.

- In order to score the highest marks, **answer all four questions as fully as you can**.

[15 marks]

2   You hear two German people talking about festivals and celebrations. What do they celebrate and how?

Listening
Track 22

Write the answers in the boxes. Answer both parts of each question.

2 a   Aaron

Celebrates...

How

[2 marks]

2 b   Kahina

Celebrates...

How

[2 marks]

3 Translate the following sentences into **English**.

3 a Er bekommt ein Geschenk.

....

.... *[2 marks]*

3 b Ich will in einer Gruppe singen.

....

.... *[2 marks]*

3 c Wir gehen joggen, aber er spielt Videospiele.

....

.... *[2 marks]*

3 d Im Zug lese ich ein Buch oder eine Zeitung.

....

.... *[2 marks]*

3 e Die berühmte Schauspielerin hat viele Preise gewonnen.

....

.... *[2 marks]*

Foundation

4 Your Swiss friend asks you about your favourite festival.
Write a short description of your favourite festival or celebration.
Write approximately **50** words in **German**.
You must write something about each bullet point.

Mention:

- when it is

- the traditions

- the music

- the food

- who you celebrate with. *[10 marks]*

Foundation

5   You read these online posts about what people do in their spare time.

> **Anja:** Ich bin kreativ und mache oft Kunst.
>
> **Rijad:** Ich schwimme gern und ich nehme regelmäßig an Wettbewerben teil.
>
> **Eleonora:** Ich bin nicht so sportlich, aber ich gehe jeden Tag spazieren.
>
> **Marvin:** Ich interessiere mich für Theater und spiele bald meine Lieblingsrolle.

Which activity does each person mention? Write the correct letter in the box.

5 a   Anja ☐

5 b   Rijad ☐

5 c   Eleonora ☐

5 d   Marvin ☐

A	cycling
B	swimming
C	drama
D	football
E	art
F	strolling

[1 mark]

[1 mark]

[1 mark]

[1 mark]

6   Translate the following sentences into **German**.

6 a   The artist is popular.

....

.... *[2 marks]*

6 b   My sister looks forward to the competition.

....

.... *[2 marks]*

6 c   I celebrated my birthday with my family.

....

.... *[2 marks]*

6 d   He would like to invite his friends to the party.

....

.... *[2 marks]*

Score: ☐

Mixed Practice — Both Tiers

1 Translate the following sentences into **German**.

Foundation

1 a I like to play football.

....

.... *[2 marks]*

1 b My favourite author has a lot of fans.

....

.... *[2 marks]*

1 c Next year he would like to take part in a match.

....

.... *[2 marks]*

1 d The wedding took place in April.

....

.... *[2 marks]*

Higher

1 e Last month we visited lots of museums to see various exhibitions.

....

.... *[2 marks]*

2 Four German celebrities are talking about what it is like to be famous.
What does each person like or dislike about being famous?
Write the correct letter in each box.

Listening
Track 23

2 a Helmut ☐

2 b Leonie ☐

2 c Tim ☐

2 d Jana ☐

A	Earning lots of money
B	People enjoying their music
C	Travelling the world
D	People being mean online
E	Having to always look good
F	Having their photo taken

[1 mark]

[1 mark]

[1 mark]

[1 mark]

3 You are writing an article for your school's magazine about celebrity culture.
Write approximately **90** words in **German**.
You must write something about each bullet point.

Describe:

- your favourite celebrity when you were younger

- what you think makes a good celebrity

- whether you would like to be famous in the future.

[15 marks]

4 You will hear 5 short sentences. Listen carefully and, using your knowledge of German sounds, write down in **German** exactly what you hear for each sentence.

Listening Track 24

You will hear each sentence **three** times: the first time as a full sentence, the second time in short sections and the third time again as a full sentence.

Use your knowledge of German sounds and grammar to make sure that what you have written makes sense. Check carefully that your spelling is accurate.

4 a Sentence 1

....

.... *[2 marks]*

4 b Sentence 2

....

.... *[2 marks]*

4 c Sentence 3

....

.... *[2 marks]*

4 d Sentence 4

....

.... *[2 marks]*

4 e Sentence 5

....

.... *[2 marks]*

Higher

5 You overhear Sven talking about a wedding he's organising.
Answer the questions in **English**.

Listening Track 25

5 a When will the wedding take place?

.... *[1 mark]*

5 b How many guests have the couple invited?

.... *[1 mark]*

5 c What have the couple asked their guests to wear?

.... *[1 mark]*

5 d Where will the wedding take place?

.... *[1 mark]*

6 You read this magazine article in which an Austrian singer, Tanja, talks about her experiences of fame. Answer the questions below in **English**.

Mein Bruder sagt mir, dass er lächelt, wenn er meine Lieder im Radio hört.
Jedoch finde ich es immer noch etwas komisch. Ich bin natürlich froh, dass Musik
meine Arbeit ist. Als Kind wollte ich immer berühmt sein. Trotzdem ist mein Leben
als Star ziemlich schwer. Obwohl meine Fans bei meinen Konzerten eine Menge
Spaß haben, fühle ich mich immer müde. Ich sorge mich jetzt um meine Gesundheit.

Ich liebe meine Fans, aber ich muss besser um mich selbst kümmern. Früher bin ich
sehr gern geschwommen, also werde ich ab jetzt in einen Schwimmverein gehen.
Auch sehe ich meine Familie nicht so viel und mein Beruf bedeutet, dass ich oft
nicht an Familienfeiern teilnehme. Deshalb werde ich mehr Zeit mit meiner Familie
verbringen. Dann werde ich vielleicht mehr Energie haben .

6 a What's it like for Tanja to hear her songs on the radio?

.... *[1 mark]*

6 b How do concerts make Tanja feel?

.... *[1 mark]*

6 c What is Tanja going to do to take care of herself? Give **two** details.

1. ....

2. .... *[2 marks]*

7 You read the website of a holiday club in Munich describing the activities they offer.

> *Möchtest du diesen Sommer an einem kreativen Club teilnehmen? Dann wird unser wochenlanger Sommer-Musikclub eine tolle Erfahrung für dich sein. Wir laden diejenigen ein, die schon ein Instrument spielen und gern ihre Leistung verbessern. Jeden Morgen leitet* ein lokaler Künstler, Larry, einen Musikkurs. Damit wirst du besser Lieder schreiben. Nachmittags wirst du dann in einer Gruppe ein Lied schreiben, das einem bestimmten Thema folgt. Wir werden das Thema den Gruppen erst am ersten Tag sagen.*
>
> *Am letzten Tag haben wir ein spannendes Fest. Jede Gruppe spielt ihr Lied und normalerweise tanzen die anderen Jugendlichen zur Musik. Wir geben auch keine Preise, deswegen kann jeder seinen Erfolg gleich genießen. Teilnehmer kommen oft allein, aber sie verlassen den Club mit neuen Freunden. Viele bleiben über viele Jahre miteinander in Kontakt und der Club wird jedes Jahr eine Tradition für sie.*
>
> *leitet = runs

Complete these sentences. Write the letter for the correct option in each box.

7 a The club is mainly aimed at students who...

A	have no musical experience.
B	want to do music professionally.
C	like developing their music skills.

[1 mark]

7 b The club-goers write a song...

A	for a local musician.
B	based on a theme.
C	for the first time.

[1 mark]

7 c On the final day, each group gets...

A	a prize.
B	to relax.
C	to perform.

[1 mark]

7 d Many of those who attend the club...

A	initially go on their own.
B	stay in contact with Larry.
C	only go for one summer.

[1 mark]

Score:

Mixed Practice — Higher

1 Spend a few minutes looking at the two photos.
Make notes on them to use during the test.

Speaking Track 13

Your teacher will ask you to talk about the content of the photos.
You should talk for approximately **one and a half minutes**.
You must say at least one thing about each photo.

Example Answer Video

After you have spoken about the content of the photos,
your teacher will then ask you questions related to
any of the topics within the theme of **Popular culture**.

[25 marks]

2 Four teenagers are talking about their favourite festivals.
Answer the following questions in **English**.

Listening Track 26

2 a What is Paula's favourite thing about Easter?

.... *[1 mark]*

2 b What is Julian most looking forward to in Vienna?

.... *[1 mark]*

2 c What does Samira's family give as gifts?

.... *[1 mark]*

2 d What does Ben do with his sister at Easter?

.... *[1 mark]*

3 You are writing an article about sport for a health and wellbeing magazine.
Write approximately **150** words in **German**.
You must write something about both bullet points.

Describe:

• whether you prefer team sports or individual sports

• a sports event you watched recently.

[25 marks]

4 You read an interview with four film stars in a culture magazine.

> **Asha:** Berühmt sein ist meiner Meinung nach eine Gelegenheit, ein Vorbild für Jugendliche zu sein und über Probleme in unserer Gesellschaft zu sprechen. Ich möchte insgesamt einen guten Einfluss auf die Welt haben.
>
> **Faysal:** Als Schauspieler kann ich meine kreativen Fähigkeiten benutzen, um verschiedene Charaktere zu entwickeln. Manchmal ist es aber schwierig, interessante Rollen zu finden, was mich unzufrieden macht.
>
> **Marcel:** Wenn ich nicht bekannt wäre, würde ich mich glücklicher fühlen. Ich kann kein normales Leben führen. Wenn ich zum Beispiel versuche, Tennis im Park zu spielen, gibt es Leute, die Fotos von mir machen wollen.
>
> **Nele:** Neulich habe ich einen Preis gewonnen und ich bin natürlich stolz darauf. Es freut mich, wenn jemand eine gute Kritik über meine Leistung schreibt. Das Gegenteil ist aber auch wahr. Scharfe Worte in negativen Kritiken können mich wirklich verletzen.

What does each person think about fame?

Write **P** for a **positive** opinion

   N for a **negative** opinion

   P + N for a **positive** and **negative** opinion.

4 a Asha

[1 mark]

4 b Faysal

[1 mark]

4 c Marcel

[1 mark]

4 d Nele

[1 mark]

5 Translate the following sentences into **English**.

5 a Im Restaurant habe ich neben meiner Tante gesessen.

....

.... *[2 marks]*

5 b Sie sagte, dass wir uns das Feuerwerk ansehen werden.

....

.... *[2 marks]*

5 c Ich bin ein großer Fan der Schauspielerin, die die Hauptrolle gespielt hat.

....

.... *[2 marks]*

5 d Silvester ist mein Lieblingsfest, weil meine Freunde und ich uns immer amüsieren.

....

.... *[2 marks]*

5 e Am Sonntag gehe ich in eine Ausstellung, um bekannte Kunstwerke zu sehen.

....

.... *[2 marks]*

6 Pia and Samuel are discussing their weekend plans.
Complete the sentences in **English**. Write **one** word in each space.

Listening
Track 27

6 a Pia is looking forward to seeing her favourite ....

on .... *[2 marks]*

6 b At the cinema, Samuel doesn't like the ....

but enjoys the .... *[2 marks]*

Score:

Where to Go, Accommodation and Travel

1　You read this text message that Ludovica has sent you on holiday.

> Hallo! Ich simse dir aus Österreich. Gestern sind wir mit dem Flugzeug hier angekommen. Ich bin im Urlaub mit meiner Familie. Ich wollte nach Frankreich fahren, aber wir werden im Winter da sein. Letzten Sommer sind wir nach Italien gereist, weil meine Großeltern dort wohnen. Das Wetter war schön und das Essen war lecker! Wir haben schon unseren nächsten Sommerurlaub geplant: im August fahren wir nach Griechenland. Wir werden in einem Hotel an der Küste wohnen.

What does Ludovica say about her holiday destinations?

Write **P** for a place she has visited **in the past**

　　　　N for a place she is visiting **now**

　　　　F for a place she will visit **in the future**.

Foundation

1 a　Austria　　☐　　　　　　　　　　　　　　*[1 mark]*

1 b　France　　☐　　　　　　　　　　　　　　*[1 mark]*

1 c　Italy　　☐　　　　　　　　　　　　　　*[1 mark]*

1 d　Greece　　☐　　　　　　　　　　　　　　*[1 mark]*

2　Three German teenagers are talking about their holiday accommodation.

Listening
Track 28

A	rude hotel staff		D	an expensive room
B	loud guests		E	an uncomfortable bed
C	a bad view		F	dirty rooms

What problem did each person have at their accommodation?

Write the correct letter in the box.

2 a　Alina　　☐　　　　　　　　　　　　　　*[1 mark]*

2 b　Joel　　☐　　　　　　　　　　　　　　*[1 mark]*

2 c　Tim　　☐　　　　　　　　　　　　　　*[1 mark]*

3 Martin and Frida are talking about their journeys to reach their holiday destinations. Answer the questions in **English**.

Listening Track 29

3 a Martin travelled by plane and which other mode of transport?

.... *[1 mark]*

3 b Why does Martin like travelling by plane? Give **one** reason.

.... *[1 mark]*

3 c Why was Martin late to the airport?

.... *[1 mark]*

Higher

3 d What was special about Frida's journey on the boat?

.... *[1 mark]*

3 e Why did Frida dislike travelling by tram?

.... *[1 mark]*

 4 You are writing a review of your recent holiday for your blog. Write approximately **150** words in **German**. You must write something about both bullet points.

Example Answer Video

Higher

Describe:

• what you liked **and** disliked about the place you visited

• your ideal holiday destination. *[25 marks]*

Score:

Find the CGP RevisionHub at cgpbooks.co.uk/haus

Section Nine — Travel and Tourism

What to Do

1 Some Swiss teenagers are describing their recent holidays.

> **Mia:** Sonnige Ferien gefallen mir sehr. Deswegen waren meine Ferien schrecklich, denn es hat die ganze Zeit geregnet.
>
> **Axel:** Ich wollte am Strand spazieren, jedoch musste ich jeden Tag langweilige historische Gebäude mit meiner Schwester besuchen.
>
> **Hamza:** Im Hotel gab es Shows nach dem Abendessen. Einige haben mir gut gefallen, aber sie waren meistens langweilig.
>
> **Katrin:** Wir haben sehr gut gegessen. Auf dem Markt gab es viel frisches Essen und alles war ziemlich billig und lecker.

What did each teenager think about their holiday?

Write **P** for a **positive** opinion

      N for a **negative** opinion

      P + N for a **positive** and **negative** opinion.

1 a Mia   ☐   *[1 mark]*

1 b Axel   ☐   *[1 mark]*

1 c Hamza   ☐   *[1 mark]*

1 d Katrin   ☐   *[1 mark]*

Foundation

---

2 When your teacher asks you, read aloud the following text in **German**.

> Im Urlaub lerne ich gern etwas Neues.
>
> Insbesondere mag ich es, die verschiedenen Traditionen eines Landes zu entdecken.
>
> Letzten Winter habe ich deshalb viele Cafés in Wien besucht.
>
> Ich wollte noch mehr machen, aber mein Bruder wollte oft im Hotel bleiben.
>
> Nächstes Jahr werde ich versuchen, irgendwo in einem Zelt zu schlafen.

> Scan the QR code to hear the teacher part of the question, or you can find the transcript in the back of the book.

Speaking Track 14

Example Answer Video

- You will then be asked four questions in **German** that relate to the topic of **Travel and tourism**.

- In order to score the highest marks, **answer all four questions as fully as you can**.

[15 marks]

Higher

3 You are writing an email to your friend who has asked for holiday advice.
Write approximately **90** words in **German**.
You must write something about each bullet point.

Describe:

•   what you did on a recent holiday

•   your opinion on what makes a good holiday

•   things you would like to do on future holidays.

[15 marks]

4 You read a letter from your pen pal, Anneliese, about holiday activities.

Im Urlaub sind meine Schwester und ich sehr aktiv. Als Kinder wollten wir immer Extremsport treiben, aber wir durften nicht, denn unsere Eltern sorgten sich um Unfälle. Jetzt machen wir immer im Urlaub aufregende Aktivitäten. Letztes Jahr gingen wir in den Bergen im Westen der USA klettern. Das war unglaublich spannend!

Bevor meine Schwester an die Universität geht, wollen meine Eltern einen letzten Familienurlaub machen. Nächsten Sommer werden wir deswegen nach Griechenland fahren und ich freue mich darauf, durch die kleine Städte spazieren zu gehen. Ich werde Zeit auf den Märkten verbringen und ich möchte versuchen, die lokale Sprache zu benutzen, aber sie ist ziemlich kompliziert.

Außerdem wollen meine Eltern an den Strand gehen, damit sie sich im Sonnenschein beim Lesen entspannen können. Wenn meine Schwester und ich mit ihnen gehen, werden wir gar nicht faul sein, sondern im Meer schwimmen gehen. Ich kann kaum warten!

Answer the following questions in **English**.

4 a Why did Anneliese's parents not allow her to do extreme sports as a child?

.... *[1 mark]*

4 b Which activity did Anneliese and her sister do in the USA last year?

.... *[1 mark]*

4 c What does Anneliese want to try to do at the markets?

.... *[1 mark]*

4 d What will Anneliese do at the beach?

.... *[1 mark]*

Score:

Higher

Technology and The Internet

1 You hear a group of young people talk about how they use their mobile devices. Complete the sentences in **English**.

Listening
Track 30

1 a Dimitri thinks downloading apps is great because...

.... *[1 mark]*

1 b Asli enjoys receiving...

.... *[1 mark]*

1 c Every night Benedikt uses his laptop to...

.... *[1 mark]*

1 d Sümeyye uses her phone to...

.... *[1 mark]*

2 Translate the following sentences into **English**.

2 a Jetzt kann man die Nachrichten auf dem Handy streamen.

....

.... *[2 marks]*

2 b Gestern habe ich etwas von einer sicheren Quelle gekauft.

....

.... *[2 marks]*

3 You are writing an article for the school newsletter about technology. Write approximately **150** words in **German**. You must write something about both bullet points.

Higher

Describe:

- the positives **and** negatives of modern technology

- what you will use the internet for next week. *[25 marks]*

4 You read these opinions about mobile phones on a forum.

Tanya: Ich weiß nicht, was ich ohne mein Handy machen würde. Es bietet mir etwas Sicherheit, wenn ich alleine unterwegs bin. Allerdings ist es auch manchmal ärgerlich. Meine Eltern wollen immer wissen, wo ich bin.

Nina: Ich finde mein Handy unbedingt praktisch. Man kann sich schnell im Internet über aktuelle Ereignisse informieren. Das Herunterladen von Musik und Videos ist auch ziemlich einfach.

Paul: Heute haben alle ein Handy. Meiner Meinung nach lebt niemand mehr in der Wirklichkeit, was komisch ist. Viele Leute sind vom Handy abhängig, weil sie ständig ihren Kontakten Nachrichten schicken wollen.

What do these people think about mobile phones?

Write **P** for a **positive** opinion

   N for a **negative** opinion

   P + N for a **positive** and **negative** opinion.

4 a Tanya ☐

[1 mark]

4 b Nina ☐

[1 mark]

4 c Paul ☐

[1 mark]

5 You are listening to a podcast. Lina is talking about her family's relationship with technology. Write the correct letter in each box.

Listening Track 31

5 a Which course has Lina's grandma recently completed?

A	a camera course
B	an internet course
C	a mobile phone course

☐

[1 mark]

5 b What does Lina's grandma want to learn next?

A	how to download photos
B	how to shop for things online
C	how to use social media

☐

[1 mark]

5 c How does Lina's brother feel about their grandma doing the course?

A	He's surprised that it was so expensive.
B	He's proud of her interest in technology.
C	He's hopeful that she will buy modern devices.

☐

[1 mark]

Score: ☐

Social Media

1 You read an article about Fanni Boom, a German influencer.

> *Bevor sie in den sozialen Medien berühmt war, war Fanni Boom total unbekannt. Jetzt folgen sieben Millionen Leute dieser Influencerin.*
>
> *Fanni Boom spricht nie über ihr privates Leben — sie lädt nur Videos über ihre Meinungen zu neuen Filmen hoch. Die Fans lieben Fanni Boom, weil sie immer witzig ist.*

Complete these sentences. Write the letter for the correct option in each box.

1 a Before she became an influencer, Fanni Boom was...

A	not famous.
B	quite famous.
C	very famous.

[1 mark]

1 b Fanni Boom uploads videos about...

A	her life.
B	cinema.
C	science.

[1 mark]

1 c People like that she is...

A	genuine.
B	funny.
C	honest.

[1 mark]

2 You are preparing a speech about social media for your German class.
Write approximately **90** words in **German**.
You must write something about each bullet point.

Describe:

- what you think of social media

- how you have used social media this week

- what you think social media will be like in the future.

[15 marks]

3 You will hear 3 short sentences. Listen carefully and, using your knowledge of German sounds, write down in **German** exactly what you hear for each sentence.

Listening
Track 32

You will hear each sentence **three** times: the first time as a full sentence, the second time in short sections and the third time again as a full sentence.

Use your knowledge of German sounds and grammar to make sure that what you have written makes sense. Check carefully that your spelling is accurate.

3 a   Sentence 1

....

....   *[2 marks]*

3 b   Sentence 2

....

....   *[2 marks]*

3 c   Sentence 3

....

....   *[2 marks]*

4   When your teacher asks you, read aloud the following text in **German**.

Speaking
Track 15

In meiner Freizeit benutze ich soziale Medien gern.

Ich lese gern die Blogs, die meine Freunde schreiben.

Manchmal nehme ich Videos auf, um mein Leben mit ihnen zu teilen.

Jedoch gibt es fremde Leute, die online gefährlich sein können.

Im Internet spreche ich nur mit meinen Freunden.

Dadurch bleibe ich sicher im Internet.

- You will then be asked four questions in **German** that relate to the topic of **Media and technology**.

- In order to score the highest marks, **answer all four questions as fully as you can**.

[15 marks]

Score:

The Home

1 You are talking to your German friend. Your teacher will play the part of your friend and will speak first.

Speaking
Track 16

• You should address your friend as *du*.

• When you see this – **?** – you will have to ask a question.

> **In order to score full marks, you must include a verb in your response to each task.**
>
>   **1.** Say **one** thing about a typical morning for you.
>
>   **2.** Say when you normally have your evening meal. (Give **one** detail.)
>
>   **3.** Give **one** opinion about your house.
>
>   **4.** Describe your bedroom. (Give **one** detail.)
>
> **? 5.** Ask your friend a question about their home.

[10 marks]

2 Friedrich is giving a tour of his house.
How does he describe each room?
Complete the table in **English**.

Listening
Track 33

hallway	kitchen	living room
narrow		

[2 marks]

3 Your German cousin has asked about your home. Write a reply.
Write approximately **90** words in **German**.
You must write something about each bullet point.

Describe:

• what your home looks like

• what rooms are in your home

• an activity you did at home recently.

[15 marks]

4   Translate the following sentences into **English**.

4 a   Unsere Wohnung ist sehr sauber.

Foundation

....

.... *[2 marks]*

4 b   Ich will schlafen, aber meine Nachbarin ist ziemlich laut.

....

.... *[2 marks]*

4 c   Neulich hat er das Fenster im Badezimmer geschlossen.

....

.... *[2 marks]*

4 d   Morgen muss ich mich daran erinnern, den Schlüssel mitzunehmen.

Higher

....

.... *[2 marks]*

5   Julia was asked about her house for a school project.
Answer the questions in **English**.

Listening
Track 34

5 a   How does Julia describe her family's farmhouse?

.... *[1 mark]*

Higher

5 b   What does Julia like about the house? Give **two** details.

1. ....

2. .... *[2 marks]*

5 c   What is wrong with the house?

.... *[1 mark]*

Score:

The Local Area, Directions and Weather

1   Noah is writing to his friend about where he lives.

> Im Stadtzentrum gibt es zwei Kinos und ein Theater. In der Nähe vom
> Theater ist der Bahnhof und gegenüber dem Bahnhof liegt das Stadion.
> Wenn es sonnig ist, gehen viele Leute an den Strand, der im Süden von
> der Stadtmitte ist. Wenn man weiter auf dem Weg vom Strand geht, kommt
> man zu einem neuen Imbiss. Neben dem Imbiss gibt es eine kleine Post.

Complete these sentences. Write the letter for the correct option in each box.

1 a   The stadium is situated...

A	to the right of the cinema.
B	opposite the railway station.
C	behind the theatre.

[1 mark]

1 b   When it is sunny, a lot of people visit...

A	the park.
B	the lake.
C	the beach.

[1 mark]

1 c   Along the path from the beach, there is a...

A	snack bar.
B	swimming pool.
C	forest.

[1 mark]

Foundation

2   Joel is talking about places in his town. What does he think about each place?

Listening
Track 35

Write **P** for a **positive** opinion

   N for a **negative** opinion

   P + N for a **positive** and **negative** opinion.

2 a   The market

[1 mark]

2 b   Clothes shops

[1 mark]

2 c   The park

[1 mark]

3 You read Marie's review of a sports shop.
Answer the following questions in **English**.

> *Ich bin in diesen Sportladen gegangen, weil ich neue Rennschuhe* kaufen wollte. Meine alten Schuhe waren nicht mehr bequem. Insgesamt war ich mit dem Laden zufrieden. Alle Schuhe waren günstig. Auch hat mir jedes Paar sehr gut gepasst. Außerdem haben die Verkäufer mir viel geholfen, meine Schuhe zu wählen. Ich würde diesen Sportladen echt empfehlen. Ich werde sicher zurückkommen!*
>
> *Rennschuhe = running shoes

3 a Why did Marie want to buy new running shoes?

.... *[1 mark]*

3 b Why was Marie happy with her shopping experience? Give **two** reasons.

1. ....

2. .... *[2 marks]*

4 You are talking to your Swiss friend. Your teacher will play the part of your friend and will speak first.

Speaking Track 17

• You should address your friend as *du*.

• When you see this – **?** – you will have to ask a question.

> **In order to score full marks, you must include a verb in your response to each task.**
>
> 1. Say what the weather is like in your area. (Give **one** detail.)
>
> 2. Say what you like to do in your area. (Give **two** details.)
>
> 3. Give **two** things that are missing in your area.
>
> 4. Say whether you would prefer to live in a village or a city. (Give **one** opinion and **one** reason.)
>
> **?** 5. Ask your friend a question about their area.

[10 marks]

Score:

The Environment

1   These Swiss teenagers are talking about local environmental problems.

> **Heike:** Die Flüsse in meiner Gegend sind schmutzig.
>
> **Bill:** Ich habe Angst vor Luftverschmutzung.
>
> **Golnar:** Ich finde die Menge von Müll schrecklich.

What does each teenager mention?

Write the correct letter in the box.

1 a   Heike   ☐

A	Traffic
B	Litter
C	Dirty rivers
D	Forests
E	Air pollution
F	Temperature

[1 mark]

1 b   Bill   ☐

[1 mark]

1 c   Golnar   ☐

[1 mark]

2   Spend a few minutes looking at the two photos.
Make notes on them to use during the test.

Your teacher will ask you to talk about the content of the photos.
You should talk for approximately **one minute**.
You must say at least one thing about each photo.

After you have spoken about the content of the photos,
your teacher will then ask you questions related to **any** of the topics
within the theme of **Communication and the world around us**.

Speaking
Track 18

Example
Answer Video

[25 marks]

3 You are writing an article for a local newspaper about environmental issues.
Write approximately **90** words in **German**.
You must write something about each bullet point.

Describe:

- an environmental issue in your local area

- what you have done recently to help protect the environment

- the effect that an environmental issue will have in the future.

[15 marks]

4 You listen to Karsten and Ida discuss pollution on their podcast.

A	Save more energy
B	Choose companies that use green energy
C	Collect litter along the river
D	Use electric vehicles
E	Reduce household waste
F	Companies stop contaminating water

Which **two** solutions does each person mention?

Write the correct letters in the boxes.

4 a Karsten ☐ ☐

[2 marks]

4 b Ida ☐ ☐

[2 marks]

Listening
Track 36

Higher

Score: ☐

Social Issues

1 Using your knowledge of grammar, complete the following sentences in **German**.
Choose the correct German word from the three options in the grid.
Write the correct **word** in the space.

Foundation

1 a .... braucht etwas Hilfe.

Du	Er	Wir

[1 mark]

1 b Du bist eine .... Frau.

reichen	reiche	reich

[1 mark]

1 c Ich habe für sie ....

stimmt	stimmen	gestimmt

[1 mark]

1 d Die Situation .... sich verbessern.

wird	werden	wirst

[1 mark]

2 You read this advert about a volunteering opportunity in a retirement home.
Answer the questions below in **English**.

> *Wir suchen einen hilfsbereiten Jugendlichen für eine freiwillige Stelle
> im Altenheim*. In der Stelle werden Sie den älteren** Menschen
> helfen. Nur zweimal pro Woche müssen Sie arbeiten und Sie wählen
> die Tage. Sie werden auch mit den älteren Menschen sprechen und
> Aktivitäten organisieren. Auch müssen Sie beim Kochen helfen.*
>
> *das Altenheim = retirement home
> **älter = elderly

2 a What quality should the young person have?

.... *[1 mark]*

2 b How often must the volunteer work in the retirement home?

.... *[1 mark]*

2 c What tasks will the volunteer do? Give **two** details.

1. ....

2. .... *[2 marks]*

3 You hear a discussion between Lena and Joel about problems in their area. Answer the questions in **English**.

Listening
Track 37

3 a What does Lena say many families can't afford in her area? Give **two** details.

.... *[2 marks]*

3 b What does Lena say some schools do to help?

.... *[1 mark]*

3 c What does Joel's volunteer group do for those in need?

.... *[1 mark]*

3 d What other problem does Joel mention?

.... *[1 mark]*

 Higher **4** You are talking to your Swiss friend. Your teacher will play the part of your friend and will speak first.

Speaking
Track 19

Example
Answer Video

- You should address your friend as *du*.

- When you see this – **?** – you will have to ask a question.

> **In order to score full marks, you must include a verb in your response to each task.**
>
> 1. Describe a time you volunteered for something. (Give **two** details.)
>
> 2. Say which social issue worries you the most and why. (Give **one** detail and **one** reason.)
>
> 3. Explain how the government can help people in need. (Give **two** details.)
>
> 4. Say **one** thing you would do to help others.
>
> **?** 5. Ask your friend a question about social issues.

[10 marks]

 Higher **5** You are writing a blog post about improving social issues. Write approximately **150** words in **German**. You must write something about both bullet points.

Describe:

- what social issues are important to you

- what you could do in the future to tackle social issues. *[25 marks]*

Score: [ ]

Mixed Practice — Foundation

Foundation

Speaking
Track 20

1 When your teacher asks you, read aloud the following text in **German**.

> Ich benutze jeden Abend das Internet.
>
> Es ist für meine Hausaufgaben sehr hilfreich.
>
> Ich lade auch Musik herunter und ich streame Videos.
>
> Soziale Medien benutze ich aber nicht so viel.
>
> Das Teilen von Fotos interessiert mich nicht.

- You will then be asked four questions in **German** that relate to the topic of **Media and technology**.

- In order to score the highest marks, **answer all four questions as fully as you can**.

[15 marks]

Foundation

2 You hear a German weather forecast on the radio.
Choose the correct answer and write the letter in each box.

Listening
Track 38

2 a On Monday, what will the weather be like in many regions?

A	sunny
B	rainy
C	windy

[1 mark]

2 b Where in the country will be warmer than other regions?

A	in the east
B	in the west
C	in the south

[1 mark]

2 c What will happen on Tuesday?

A	The temperature will fall.
B	There will be stormy weather.
C	It will reach 25 degrees.

[1 mark]

3 You see this photo on social media.
What's in this photo?
Write **five** sentences in **German**.

Foundation

3 a .... *[2 marks]*

3 b .... *[2 marks]*

3 c .... *[2 marks]*

3 d .... *[2 marks]*

3 e .... *[2 marks]*

4 Some German teenagers are giving their opinions about their town.

> **Alma:** Im Stadtzentrum gibt es immer viel Verkehr auf den Straßen und ich finde es schrecklich.
> Ich denke, dass es gefährlich für die Umwelt und für die Kinder in der Stadt ist.
> **Fynn:** In der Haupteinkaufsstraße gibt es viele tolle Geschäfte. Am Wochenende gehe
> ich gern mit meiner Schwester einkaufen, weil wir zusammen viel Spaß haben.
> **Naim:** Ich finde unsere Stadt sehr schön, denn im Zentrum gibt es viele historische Gebäude.
> Auch gehe ich gern mit meinem Hund im großen öffentlichen Park spazieren,
> jedoch darf ich ihn nicht in die Geschäfte mitnehmen.

Match the correct person with each of the following questions.

Write **A** for **Alma**

    F for **Fynn**

    N for **Naim**.

Write the correct letter in each box.

Foundation

4 a Who likes the shops in the town?

☐ *[1 mark]*

4 b Who thinks the centre of town is beautiful?

☐ *[1 mark]*

4 c Who thinks there is a lot of traffic on the roads?

☐ *[1 mark]*

4 d Who worries about children's safety in town?

☐ *[1 mark]*

4 e Who enjoys the green spaces?

☐ *[1 mark]*

5 Using your knowledge of grammar, complete the following sentences in **German**.
Choose the correct German word from the three options in the grid.
Write the correct **word** in the space.

5 a Umweltverschmutzung ist ein .... Problem.

große	großes	großer

[1 mark]

5 b Gehst du in .... Küche?

den	dem	die

[1 mark]

5 c Ich .... nach Spanien gereist.

bin	bist	sind

[1 mark]

5 d Jeden Tag benutzt .... den Laptop.

wir	ich	er

[1 mark]

6 You hear Stella give a presentation about tourism in her local area.
Answer the questions in **English**.

Listening
Track 39

6 a Where is Stella's hometown located?

.... *[1 mark]*

6 b When is the town popular with tourists?

.... *[1 mark]*

6 c Why are tourists important for the town?

.... *[1 mark]*

6 d What does Stella say is a disadvantage of tourism in her town?

.... *[1 mark]*

7 Translate the following sentences into **English**.

7 a Sie teilt einen Post.

....

.... *[2 marks]*

7 b Wir recyceln immer unsere alte Kleidung.

....

.... *[2 marks]*

7 c Meine Wohnung hat drei Zimmer, aber es gibt keinen Garten.

....

.... *[2 marks]*

7 d Im Moment bin ich arbeitslos, also suche ich eine Stelle.

....

.... *[2 marks]*

7 e Letztes Jahr habe ich in einem billigen Hotel gewohnt.

....

.... *[2 marks]*

8 Your Swiss pen pal has asked you about holidays.
Write a short description of your favourite place to go on holiday.
Write approximately **50** words in **German**.
You must write something about each bullet point.

Mention:

• the location

• how you get there

• the weather

• the accommodation

• activities you do there. *[10 marks]*

Score:

Mixed Practice — Both Tiers

LISTENING

1 Wanda and Manuel are talking about how they help their local community.

Which **two** activities does each person mention?

Write the correct letters in the boxes.

A	planting trees
B	raising money
C	social media campaigns
D	babysitting
E	helping old people
F	litter picking

Listening Track 40

1 a Wanda ☐ ☐

[2 marks]

1 b Manuel ☐ ☐

[2 marks]

WRITING

2 Your Austrian friend has asked you about where you live.
Write approximately **90** words in **German**.
You must write something about each bullet point.

Describe:

• something you did in your local area recently

• a social issue in your local area

• what you think your local area will be like in the future.

[15 marks]

READING

3 You see some headlines in a German local newspaper.

A	Temperaturen in der Region sind höher als im letzten Jahr.
B	Die Mehrheit ist für mehr Häuser in der Gegend.
C	Buslinien im Stadtzentrum werden bald besser.
D	Online-Mobbing steigt unter Jugendlichen.
E	Kunden geben weniger Geld in der Haupteinkaufsstraße aus.

Which headline matches each topic?

Write the correct letter in each box.

3 a Public transport ☐

[1 mark]

3 b Accommodation ☐

[1 mark]

3 c Local businesses ☐

[1 mark]

4 Translate the following sentences into **German**.

4 a My mobile phone is broken.

....

.... *[2 marks]*

4 b Yesterday I ordered a new dress online.

....

.... *[2 marks]*

4 c Trains are more environmentally friendly than planes.

....

.... *[2 marks]*

4 d The scientist warned us about climate change.

....

.... *[2 marks]*

5 You will hear 3 short sentences. Listen carefully and, using your knowledge of German sounds, write down in **German** exactly what you hear for each sentence.

Listening
Track 41

You will hear each sentence **three** times: the first time as a full sentence, the second time in short sections and the third time again as a full sentence.

Use your knowledge of German sounds and grammar to make sure that what you have written makes sense. Check carefully that your spelling is accurate.

5 a **Sentence 1**

....

.... *[2 marks]*

5 b **Sentence 2**

....

.... *[2 marks]*

5 c **Sentence 3**

....

.... *[2 marks]*

6   You read this email from your friend Adrian about his recent holiday.

Example
Answer Video

> Letzte Woche war ich in einer englischen Stadt. Ich habe in einem Hotel gewohnt, das direkt in der Hauptstraße war, deshalb hatte ich keine Ruhe. Außerdem war das Zimmer echt teuer, aber es war sauber und bequem.
>
> Oft gab es kein WLAN, also konnte ich den Weg durch die Stadt auf meinem Handy nicht suchen. Jedoch haben viele hilfsbereite Menschen mir den richtigen Weg beschrieben.
>
> Ich habe so viele tolle Dinge gesehen und süße Andenken* gekauft. Ich habe aber nur wenige Fotos gemacht und das ist schade.
>
> In der Stadt war Wasserverschmutzung ein Problem. In meiner Stadt sind die Leute umweltfreundlicher, deshalb ist der Fluss nicht so schmutzig. Trotzdem war die Luft echt frisch, denn man durfte nicht mit dem Auto im Stadtzentrum fahren.
>
> *Andenken = souvenirs

Complete these sentences. Write the letter for the correct option in each box.

6 a   Adrian thought his hotel...

A	was really quiet.
B	gave him a nice room.
C	was well-priced.

[1 mark]

6 b   Adrian found it hard to...

A	connect to the internet.
B	buy a new phone.
C	speak to the locals.

[1 mark]

6 c   Adrian wished that he had...

A	spent less money.
B	seen more things.
C	taken more photos.

[1 mark]

6 d   Adrian says his home city has cleaner...

A	water.
B	air.
C	streets.

[1 mark]

Score:

Mixed Practice — Higher

1 Spend a few minutes looking at the two photos.
Make notes on them to use during the test.

Speaking
Track 21

Your teacher will ask you to talk about the content of the photos.
You should talk for approximately **one and a half minutes**.
You must say at least one thing about each photo.

After you have spoken about the content of the photos,
your teacher will then ask you questions related to **any** of the topics
within the theme of **Communication and the world around us**.

[25 marks]

2 You hear Lola and Max talking about problems in society.
Complete the sentences in **English**.

Listening
Track 42

2 a Max thinks that the effect of hunger is...

.... *[1 mark]*

2 b Max says that the German population should...

.... *[1 mark]*

2 c Last week, Lola...

.... *[1 mark]*

2 d According to Max, governments should...

.... *[1 mark]*

WRITING

3   Translate the following sentences into **German**.

Example Answer Video

3 a   Climate change is dangerous for the environment.

....

....   *[2 marks]*

3 b   The kitchen is the biggest room in our house.

....

....   *[2 marks]*

Higher

3 c   We drive into town in order to go shopping.

....

....   *[2 marks]*

3 d   I'm not sure whether I should buy a computer.

....

....   *[2 marks]*

3 e   I never travel in Europe without recording lots of videos.

....

....   *[2 marks]*

LISTENING

4   Three Swiss teenagers are talking about using the internet.

Listening Track 43

Write **P** if they did the activity **in the past**

     N if they do the activity **now**

     F if they will do the activity **in the future**.

Answer all parts of question 4.

Higher

4 a   Jonas — playing video games   ☐

[1 mark]

4 b   Livia — writing blog posts   ☐

[1 mark]

4 c   Sabri — reading the news   ☐

[1 mark]

5 Read this article about biodiversity. Answer the questions in **English**.

Higher

Seit 2000 ist der 22. Mai der Internationale Tag der biologischen Vielfalt*. Das Ziel des Tages ist, die Menschen besser über die biologische Vielfalt zu informieren. An diesem Tag gibt es in Ländern auf der ganzen Welt verschiedene Veranstaltungen, darunter Projekte und Diskussionen. Die biologische Vielfalt ist für unsere Welt extrem wichtig. Viele Tiere sind seit langem in höchster Gefahr und leider sterben jedes Jahr immer mehr Tierarten aus.

Das Problem hat viele Ursachen. Die Industrie kann Tieren und Pflanzen wirklich schaden. Wegen der Waldzerstörung verschwinden im Moment Gebiete, wo viele Tiere leben. Manche glauben auch, dass der Klimawandel die biologische Vielfalt reduziert. Am Internationalen Tag der biologischen Vielfalt denkt man darüber nach, was man tun kann, um die Umwelt zu schützen. Wenn Regierungen zusammenarbeiten, ist es vielleicht möglich, Lösungen zu finden.

*die biologische Vielfalt = biological diversity

---

5 a What is the aim of the International Day for Biological Diversity?

.... *[1 mark]*

5 b What negative development has there been for biodiversity?

.... *[1 mark]*

5 c What is causing this development? Give **two** details.

1. ....

2. .... *[2 marks]*

6 You are writing an article about tourism.
Write approximately **150** words in **German**.
You must write something about both bullet points.

Higher

Describe:

• the positive **and** negative impacts of tourism

• how you will be more environmentally friendly on your next holiday. *[25 marks]*

Score:

Nouns

1   Underline the noun or nouns in each sentence below.

a   Die Eier sind auf dem Tisch.

b   Ich finde Tennis langweilig.

c   Mein Bruder und ich lesen gern Krimis.

d   Das blaue Kleid gefällt meiner Schwester.

e   Mein Cousin kauft ein Eis.

f   Es gibt keine Moschee in meiner Stadt.

g   Heute scheint die Sonne.

h   Sophie isst viel Kuchen.

i   Dein Freund hat ein neues Auto.

j   Herr Meyer fliegt nach Spanien.

k   Meine Sportschuhe sind grün.

l   Wo ist meine Handtasche?

2   Write **M**, **F** or **N** after each group of nouns to show whether they are masculine, feminine or neuter.

a   Deutschland   England   Frankreich   ....

b   Ärztin   Polizistin   Lehrerin   ....

c   Montag   Dienstag   Freitag   ....

d   Sommer   Winter   Frühling   ....

e   Lesen   Schwimmen   Fernsehen   ....

f   Meinung   Beziehung   Umgebung   ....

g   Mannschaft   Wissenschaft   Landschaft   ....

h   Gesundheit   Vergangenheit   Freiheit   ....

i   Buchverkäufer   Hotelchef   Physiklehrer   ....

j   Kunstmuseum   Kinopublikum   Stadtzentrum   ....

H̄ **k**   Bäumchen   Liebchen   Kätzchen   ....

3   Write out the plural forms of these nouns.

a   die Wurst   ....

b   das Lied   ....

c   die Rolle   ....

d   der Zahn   ....

e   das Kind   ....

f   das Café   ....

g   der Tag   ....

h   die Einladung   ....

i   die Stunde   ....

j   der Bruder   ....

k   das Haus   ....

l   das Bett   ....

4 Circle the correct form of the noun in **bold** to complete these sentences.

a   Der **Junge** / **Jungen** geht ins Kino.

b   Ich gebe den **Mensch** / **Menschen** das Geld.

c   Die Dame besucht die **Herren** / **Herr**.

d   Wir sehen die **Jungen** / **Junge** auf der Straße.

e   Das Mädchen spielt Fußball mit den **Junge** / **Jungen**.

f   Wie ist dein **Name** / **Namen**?

5 Translate these sentences into **English**.

a   Er spricht sehr gut Französisch.

   ....

b   Das Joggen ist eine beliebte Aktivität.

   ....

6 Complete these sentences by turning the adjectives in **bold** into nouns.

Example: Die ...._Alten_......... wohnen in der Nähe.   **alt**

a   Die .... kochen besonders gut.   **deutsch**

b   Die .... gehen in die Grundschule.   **klein**

c   Ich mag die ....   **freundlich**

d   Wie kennst du die .... ?   **nett**

7 Translate these sentences into **German**.

a   Tell me the bad thing first.

   ....

b   She expects a lot of good.

   ....

c   I will do something crazy.

   ....

Cases and Articles

1   Underline the subject or subjects in each sentence below.

a   Ich gehe ins Kino.

b   Mein Bruder mag Tischtennis.

c   Wir haben einen Hund gesehen.

d   Mein Vater isst einen Kuchen.

e   Gestern habe ich Basketball gespielt.

f   Wann besuchst du deine Tante?

g   Mein Freund ist sehr komisch.

h   Habt ihr schon gegessen?

i   Fußball ist langweilig.

j   Meine Mutter und ich gehen einkaufen.

k   Frankreich ist ein schönes Land.

l   Jeden Morgen singt der Vogel.

2   Underline the word or words in the accusative case in the sentences below.

a   Lara hat eine Hose gekauft.

b   Ich trage sehr oft ein T-Shirt.

c   Das Auto da will ich haben.

d   Meine Eltern sprechen Spanisch.

e   Ich habe Kaffee mitgebracht.

f   Wir benutzen oft soziale Medien.

g   Mario hat eine E-Mail geschrieben.

h   Zusammen sehen wir einen Film.

i   Möchten Sie ein Glas Cola trinken?

j   Du musst deine Hausaufgaben machen.

k   Ich habe mein Handy zu Hause vergessen.

l   Mathe finde ich sehr langweilig.

3   Write down whether the words in **bold** are in the **nominative**, the **accusative** or the **dative** case.

a   Ich esse **den Kuchen** zum Frühstück.

....

b   Ben schreibt **seinem Freund** einen Brief.

....

> The nominative case is used for the person or thing doing the action.

c   Er kauft immer **Obst**.

....

d   **Suzi** sieht jeden Abend einen Film.

....

e   Ich helfe **meinem Freund** mit den Hausaufgaben.

....

> The accusative case is used for the person or thing the action is being done to.

f   Ich singe meinem Freund **ein schönes Lied**.

....

g   Ich habe **das Eis** weggeworfen.

....

h   **Sie** trinkt das Wasser.

....

i   **Er** gibt seiner Freundin ein Geschenk.

....

> The dative case is used for the person or thing that is indirectly affected by the action.

j   Ich schreibe **meiner Oma** jeden Tag eine SMS.

....

k   Am Wochenende spielen wir **Fußball**.

....

4 Add an 'n' to the words in the sentences below where it is needed.

Higher

a Ich gebe meinen Brüder...... die Bücher...... .

b Der Lehrer hilft den Studente...... mit ihren Probleme...... .

5 Circle the correct words in **bold** to complete the sentences below.

Higher

a Ich treffe die Freundin **meines Bruders** / **meinem Bruder**.

b Ich schreibe **meines Freundes** / **meinem Freund** eine E-Mail.

6 Fill in the gaps with the correct **German** word for 'the'. The cases are given in **bold**.

Example: ....*Die*.... Katze schläft auf dem Bett. **nominative**

a Ich mag .... Hund. **accusative**

b Ich singe .... Hund ein Lied. **dative**

c Er sieht .... Tier im Garten. **accusative**

d .... Club fängt bald an. **nominative**

e Ich gebe .... Katzen Fisch. **dative**

H f Die Farbe .... Autos ist rot. **genitive**

7 Complete the sentences by using the correct **German** forms of 'the' and 'a'.

a .... (the) Erwachsenen kaufen .... (a) neues Haus.

b Mein Hund spielt mit .... (the) Ball.

c .... (the) Mädchen sieht jede Woche .... (a) neuen Film.

d Er besucht .... (a) Museum in .... (the) Stadtmitte.

H e .... (the) Wände .... (of the) Schlafzimmers sind grün.

8 Complete these sentences with the correct form of the words in brackets.

Example: Gestern habe ich ....*kein*.... (no) Gemüse gegessen.

a Ich habe .... (a) Hund, aber .... (no) Katze.

b In meiner Stadt gibt es .... (no) Kino und .... (no) Bahnhof.

c .... (no) Freunde haben mich besucht, als ich krank war.

d Ich will .... (a) Kaffee trinken, aber es gibt .... (no) Café.

H e Sie stiehlt die Jacke .... Mannes (the) und ich stehle die Milch .... Katze (a).

Pronouns and Word Order

1   Fill in the gaps in the second sentences with the correct pronouns to match the nouns in **bold**.

Example: Der Junge ist nett. __Er__ ist mein Freund.

a   **Der Hund** ist schwarz. .... heißt Max.

b   **Die Kinder** gehen nicht in die Schule. .... spielen im Garten.

c   **Das Haus** ist modern. .... liegt auf der Hauptstraße.

d   **Marie** ist meine beste Freundin. .... ist sehr witzig.

2   Write down the correct **German** form of the word 'you' to use in the following situations.

a   Saying to your teacher: 'Could you explain that again, please?' ....

b   Asking a few friends: 'Would you like to come to my party?' ....

c   Arranging to meet a friend at the cinema: 'Can you meet me at 7 pm?' ....

d   Asking your friend's parents: 'Did you enjoy your holiday?' ....

3   Circle the correct pronoun in **bold** to complete the sentences.

a   Du hilfst **sie / ihr**.

b   Meine Katze liebt **mich / mir** sehr.

c   Ich habe **ihn / ihm** gesehen.

d   Ich danke **Sie / Ihnen**.

e   Sie gibt **mich / mir** das Buch.

f   Ich werde **dich / dir** ein Lied singen.

g   Er spricht mit **wir / uns** über **ihr / euch**.

h   Hast du **sie / ihnen** eingeladen?

4   Translate these sentences into **German**.

a   Someone visited me yesterday.

....

b   She saw no one in the shop.

....

5   Choose the correct relative pronoun from the box to complete the sentences.

a   Die Studentin, ... Deutsch spricht, ist glücklich.

b   Das Baby, ... immer weint, ist sehr klein.

c   Ich kenne den Schüler, ... zu dieser Schule geht.

der
die
das

Section Thirteen — Nouns, Cases and Linking Words

6 Circle the correct pronoun in **bold** to complete the sentences.

a Der Mann, **der** / **den** ich gestern besucht habe, ist krank.

b Gibt es etwas, **was** / **der** ich wissen sollte?

c Ich habe mit der Frau gesprochen, **die** / **der** ich liebe.

d Das Buch, **was** / **das** sie im Moment liest, ist interessant.

e Wir bleiben hier, **wo** / **die** es heiß ist.

7 Complete the sentences using the correct interrogative pronoun from the box.

> wen   wem   wem   wer   wen   wer

a .... wohnt in deinem Haus?

b Mit .... sprichst du?

c .... spielt Fußball?

d .... hilfst du?

e Für .... kaufst du das?

f .... hast du besucht?

8 Complete the sentences by adding the correct reflexive pronouns.

a Ich freue .... sehr auf meinen Geburtstag.

b Mein Freund fühlt .... sehr kalt. Er hat .... nicht warm genug angezogen.

c Wir haben .... heute Morgen bewegt.

d Ihr interessiert .... für Geschichte. Sie interessieren .... für Mathe.

e Ich kann .... nicht vorstellen, ohne mein Handy zu sein.

H

f Du kannst .... dieses teure Auto nicht leisten.

9 Rewrite these groups of words to form correct sentences.
There's more than one right answer for each group.

a ich Basketball spiele am Freitag ....

b am Samstag ich spiele Tennis ....

c ich werde besuchen Frankreich im Juli ....

d im August werde ich reisen nach Frankreich ....

e ich fahre mit dem Bus am Montag in die Schule ....

f am Dienstag fahre ich in die Schule mit dem Fahrrad ....

Conjunctions and Prepositions

1 These sentences have the wrong conjunctions in them. Choose the correct conjunction from the box — use each one only **once**.

| und aber denn oder |

   a Was magst du lieber — Cola aber Kaffee? ....

   b Ich möchte ein Kilo Zucker denn sechs Eier. ....

   c Wir gehen wandern, oder die Sonne scheint. ....

   d Sie will ihren Freund sehen, und er ist krank. ....

2 Join up each pair of sentences using the conjunction in **bold**.

   a Ich bleibe zu Hause. Das Wetter ist schlecht. **wenn**

    ....

   b Er fährt in den Urlaub. Er hat kein Geld. **obwohl**

    ....

   c Meine Mutter hat sehr gut gesungen. Sie war jünger. **als**

    ....

   d Sie lernt jeden Abend. Sie hat Prüfungen im Mai. **weil**

    ....

Higher   **e** Ich studiere Deutsch. Ich kann in München arbeiten. **damit**

    ....

3 Translate these sentences into **English**.

   a Du kannst entweder Hähnchen oder Fisch essen.

    ....

Higher   **b** Sie lernt gern sowohl Erdkunde als auch Geschichte.

    ....

   c Er spielt weder Basketball noch Fußball.

    ....

4 Complete the sentences using the correct words from the box — use each word only **once**.

| von | durch | mit | gegen | bis | für | ohne | nach | über | zur |

a Ich werde von fünfzehn Uhr .... siebzehn Uhr warten.

b .... der Schule werde ich .... den Wald spazieren.

c West Ham spielt .... Hull. Wer wird gewinnen?

d Dieser Brief ist .... meiner Schwester. Ist er .... mich?

e Ich bin .... meine Tasche .... Schule gekommen.

f Ich spreche .... meinen Freunden .... Politik.

5 Circle the correct word in **bold** to complete the sentences.

Hint: the case will depend on whether there's movement or not.

a Ich gehe **ins** / **im** Kino.

b Der Junge steht an **die** / **der** Tür.

c Ich bleibe **ins** / **im** Hotel.

d Sie gehen an **den** / **dem** Strand.

e Ich sitze auf **den** / **dem** Boden.

Higher

f Ich fahre über **die** / **der** Brücke.

g Wir treffen uns vor **das** / **dem** Restaurant.

h Er geht hinter **das** / **dem** Auto.

i Die Katze läuft unter **den** / **dem** Tisch.

j Das Haus ist neben **eine** / **einer** Synagoge.

Higher

6 Complete the sentences using the correct words from the box — use each one only **once**.

a .... seiner Verletzung spielt er noch Fußball.

b .... der Woche gehe ich nicht in die Stadt.

c .... des Schnees bleibt er heute zu Hause.

d .... eines Handys kauft er einen neuen Laptop.

| während |
| wegen |
| trotz |
| statt |

7 Translate these sentences into **German**.

a There is a table in the garden and a bird sits on it.

....

Higher

b He is a shop assistant and, in addition, works in a café.

....

c While cooking, I always listen to music.

....

Adjectives

1   Complete the sentences by translating the words in **bold** into **German**.

    a   Mein Bruder ist ....   **stupid**

    b   Ich finde Mathe ....   **boring**

    c   Meine Oma ist ....   **funny**

    d   Das Gebäude ist ....   **big**

2   Complete the sentences with the correct adjective endings.

    a   Die braun..... Katze schläft auf dem grün..... Stuhl neben dem weiß..... Tisch.

    b   Die klein..... Kinder spielen mit dem groß..... Hund in dem schön..... Park.

    c   Sie findet die schwarz..... Schuhe und das rot..... T-Shirt von dem alt..... Mann.

    d   Ich gebe dem klein..... Mädchen den lecker..... Kuchen und das frisch..... Obst.

  H **e**   Das gelb..... Auto gehört der groß..... Frau mit den blau..... Augen.

3   Complete the sentences with the correct adjective endings.

    a   Ein schwarz..... Hund spielt mit einem rot..... Ball in einem schön..... Garten.

    b   Ich gebe meiner nett..... Schwester ein alt..... Kleid und einen neu..... Rock.

    c   Ich habe keine gut..... Freunde in meiner neu..... Schule.

    d   Ich schreibe meinem best..... Freund eine lang..... E-Mail und einen kurz..... Brief.

4   Translate the following phrases into **German**, using the correct adjective endings.

    a   two red cars   ....   **c**   green bags   ....

    b   few hot days   ....   **d**   some small dogs   ....

5   Complete the table of the possessive adjective '**mein**', using the correct endings.

	Masculine	Feminine	Neuter	Plural
Nominative	*mein*			*meine*
Accusative		*meine*	*mein*	
Dative				
H Genitive				

6   Circle the correct form of the word in **bold** to complete the sentences below.

    a   **Welcher** / **Welchen** Zug fährt nach Köln?

    b   **Diese** / **Dieser** Kuchen sind lecker.

    c   In **welcher** / **welche** Stadt hast du studiert?

    d   Sie besuchen **unser** / **unserem** Haus.

    e   Bist du **letzter** / **letzte** Woche zur Party gegangen?

    f   **Dein** / **Deinen** neuer Freund ist sehr komisch.

7   Translate these sentences into **German**.

    a   Have you drunk a lot of water?

    ....

    b   I have drunk little water today.

    ....

8   Finish off these sentences with the comparative form of the adjective in **bold**.

    Example: Der Hund ist **klein**, aber die Katze ist ....*kleiner*........... .

    a   Mein Auto ist **langsam**, aber dein Auto ist ....

    b   Dieser Film ist **gut**, aber der andere Film ist ....

    c   Meine Oma ist **alt**, aber mein Opa ist ....

    d   Die Pflanze ist **groß**, aber der Baum ist ....

    e   Der Park ist **nah**, aber das Geschäft ist ....

9   Complete these sentences with the superlative form of the adjective in **bold**.

    Example: Hannah ist sehr **klein**. Sie ist ....*die kleinste*........... Teilnehmerin.

    a   Alex ist sehr **schnell**. Sie ist .... Schülerin.

    b   Klaus ist immer **traurig**. Er ist ....

    c   Mein Opa ist wirklich **alt**. Er ist ....

    d   Dieses Kino ist nicht besonders **nah**. Wo ist .... Kino?

    e   Das Hemd ist super **bunt**. Es ist .... Kleidungsstück.

    f   Die Synagoge ist sehr **hoch**. Sie ist .... Gebäude.

Higher

Adverbs

1 Translate these sentences into **English**.

a Er singt schlecht. Sie tanzt gut.

....

b Ich fahre langsam und du sprichst viel.

....

c Mein Bruder arbeitet hart und schwimmt schnell.

....

d Normalerweise ist er ziemlich faul. Leider wird er bestimmt zu spät kommen.

....

2 Use a **German** adverb to fill the gap in each of these sentences and match the English translation.

a Er spielt .... Basketball. *He plays basketball badly.*

b Ich laufe sehr .... um den Platz. *I run very slowly around the pitch.*

c Du singst .... *You sing beautifully.*

d Der Film war .... gut. *The film was really good.*

e Sie lacht sehr .... *She laughs very happily.*

f .... hat es angefangen zu regnen. *Suddenly it started to rain.*

3 Translate these sentences into **German**.

a Sometimes the sun shines, but recently it has rained a lot.

....

b The train is always late. I hope that it is on time next week.

....

c Have you already eaten in this restaurant? I was here yesterday evening.

....

4 Complete the sentences with the **German** translations of the adverbial phrases given in **bold**.

Example: Ich habe ihn ....*gestern*........ nicht besucht. **yesterday**

a Es ist sehr laut in der Stadtmitte, weil es .... Menschen gibt. **everywhere**

b Es gibt .... ein schönes Café. **there**

c .... kommt mein Freund mich besuchen. **tomorrow**

d Ich bin mir sicher, ich habe sie .... gesehen. **somewhere**

e Mein Bruder fährt .... nach London. **on Wednesdays**

f Es ist wirklich schön, wieder .... in Heidelberg zu sein. **here**

5 Translate these sentences into **English**.

a Al spricht lauter als Eoin. ....

b Rhys tanzt genauso gut wie Faiz. ....

c Sami lächelt nicht so oft wie Aled. ....

d Jo mag Tennis genauso viel wie Pete. ....

6 Finish off these sentences with the comparative form of the adverb in **bold**.

Example: Ich schwimme **oft**, aber sie schwimmen ....*öfter*........ .

a Thomas fährt **langsam**, aber Anna fährt ....

b Ich schreibe **schlecht**, aber er schreibt ....

c Er läuft **viel**, aber sie läuft ....

d Du singst **gut**, aber sie singt ....

e Meine Oma liest **gern**, aber sie sieht .... fern.

7 Complete the sentences with the **German** translations of the superlatives given in **bold**.

a Ich mag Geschichte, aber Englisch gefällt mir .... **the best**

b Tanzen macht Spaß, aber ich gehe .... ins Kino. **most preferably**

c Ich komme .... mit dem Bus in die Stadt. **the quickest**

d Du hast viele Geschenke, aber ich habe .... **the most**

e Sie singt schrecklich und ich singe .... **the most terribly**

f Meine Schwester macht Training .... **the most often**

Higher

Present Tense & More Ways to Use Verbs

1 Write out the correct present tense form of each verb to match the person given.

a hören — ich   ....

b lernen — wir   ....

c lieben — er   ....

d sagen — ihr   ....

e schicken — Sie   ....

f reden — sie *(sing.)* ....

g schlagen — ich   ....

h bringen — du   ....

i studieren — wir   ....

j trinken — ihr   ....

k stellen — sie *(pl.)* ....

l suchen — du   ....

2 Write out the correct present tense form of each verb to match the person given.

a feiern — ich   ....

b feiern — sie *(sing.)* ....

c wandern — Sie   ....

d wandern — du   ....

e sammeln — man   ....

f sammeln — ich   ....

g lächeln — ihr   ....

h lächeln — wir   ....

3 Translate the sentences into **German**.

a Riyam is playing football. ....

b My brother is writing an email. ....

c My father works on Saturdays. ....

d Christopher is swimming today. ....

H e I've been living here for five years. ....

4 Write the present tense forms of the verb **sein** — to be.

a ich   ....

b du   ....

c er / sie / es / man   ....

d wir   ....

e ihr   ....

f Sie / sie   ....

5 Write the present tense forms of the verb **haben** — to have.

a ich   ....

b du   ....

c er / sie / es / man   ....

d wir   ....

e ihr   ....

f Sie / sie   ....

6 Write the present tense forms of the verb **wissen** — to know.

a ich .... **d** wir ....

b du .... **e** ihr ....

c er / sie / es / man .... **f** Sie / sie ....

7 Fill in the gaps with the correct form of the verb in **bold**.

a Meine Freundin .... jeden Tag Pommes. **essen**

b Der Polizist .... gern in seinem Polizeiauto. **fahren**

c Wie .... du das Essen? **finden**

d Mein Vater .... die Zeitung. **lesen**

8 Write **A** or **D** after each verb to show whether they are followed by the accusative or dative case.

a helfen .... **c** folgen .... **e** glauben .... **g** antworten ....

b tragen .... **d** wissen .... **f** lesen .... **h** geben ....

9 Translate the sentences into **German** using an **impersonal verb** in each one.

a It's raining today. ....

b There are three buildings. ....

c I like it here in Berlin. ....

d I am not so well. ....

10 Translate these passive sentences into **German** using '**man**' and an active verb.

a The chicken was eaten. ....

b The bike was stolen. ....

11 Rearrange the words to form sentences using infinitive constructions.

Example: gehe laufen Ich um zu bleiben in Form   *Ich gehe laufen, um in Form zu bleiben.*

a versucht Spanisch Er lernen zu ....

b Geld verdienen Wir um zu arbeiten ....

c zu nie draußen Brille nach tragen Ich ohne eine gehe ....

d statt klettern gehen zu Sie ihre Hausaufgaben machen ....

Past Tense

1   Give the **German** infinitives and past participles of the verbs below.

Example: to look for ......_suchen, gesucht_......

a	to make	....	**h**	to eat	....
b	to believe	....	**i**	to work	....
c	to need	....	**j**	to explain	....
d	to buy	....	**k**	to use	....
e	to ask	....	**l**	to try	....
f	to choose	....	**m**	to lose	....
g	to visit	....	**n**	to take	....

2   Give the **German** infinitives that go with the past participles.

Example: gelaufen ...._laufen_...........

a	geblieben	....	**g**	gesprochen	....
b	gewesen	....	**h**	gefunden	....
c	passiert	....	**i**	gebracht	....
d	gefolgt	....	**j**	verstanden	....
e	gegangen	....	**k**	spaziert	....
f	geflogen	....	**l**	bezahlt	....

3   Translate the sentences into **German** using the perfect tense.

a   I went to Munich. ....

b   He ate a cake. ....

c   We visited a museum. ....

d   He stayed in bed. ....

e   The plane flew quickly. ....

f   When did you come to the shop? ....

g   We arrived at two o'clock. ....

h   The cat drank a lot of milk. ....

4 Write the simple past forms of the verb **sein** — to be.

a ich ....

d wir ....

b du ....

e ihr ....

c er / sie / es / man ....

f Sie / sie ....

5 Write the simple past forms of the verb **haben** — to have.

a ich ....

d wir ....

b du ....

e ihr ....

c er / sie / es / man ....

f Sie / sie ....

6 Complete the sentences by adding the correct simple past verb endings.

a Wir mach......... zu viel Lärm und stör......... unsere Nachbarn.

b Mein Vater kauf......... ein neues Haus und ich kauf......... ein neues Auto.

c Mein Opa arbeite......... als Verkäufer. Meine Eltern arbeite......... als Lehrer.

d Du spiel......... ein Instrument und besuch......... viele Konzerte.

e Wir lieb......... Musik und ihr lieb......... Filme.

f Als ich jung war, hass......... ich Gemüse. Meine Geschwister hass......... Obst.

7 Give the correct simple past form of these irregular verbs. Match the person given.

Example: singen — ich *ich sang* ....

a kommen — ich ....

f nehmen — ihr ....

b laufen — er ....

g geben — ich ....

c helfen — ich ....

h schreiben — er ....

d sehen — du ....

i wissen — du ....

e denken — sie *(pl.)* ....

j gehen — wir ....

8 Translate the sentences below into **German** using the simple past.

a I drove to Cologne and sang in the church.

....

b We ate fast food, drank cola and watched TV.

....

Talking about the Future & Negative Forms

1 Translate the sentences below into **German** using the present tense.

a This summer, we are going to go swimming every day.

....

b I am buying a house next year.

....

c Tomorrow I am drinking only water.

....

2 Complete the sentences in the future tense using the correct form of **werden**.

a Du .... morgen in die Schule gehen.

b Susi und du, ihr .... zusammen ins Kino gehen.

c Susi .... um halb acht hier sein.

d Ich .... um halb sieben aufstehen.

e Wir .... Brot essen und Kaffee trinken.

f Deine Freunde .... in der Klasse sein.

g Deine neue Lehrerin .... sehr nett sein.

h .... Sie den ganzen Tag warten?

3 Translate the sentences below into **German** using **werden** and the correct infinitives.

a Next year, I'm going to do lots of sport and play tennis regularly.

....

b Next week, Andre will travel into town by bus.

....

c This summer, there will be lots of good films.

....

4 Translate the sentences into **English**.

a Hast du heute nichts gemacht?

....

b Sie hat mir nie die lustige Geschichte erzählt.

....

c Er ist gestern nicht an die Küste gefahren.

....

5 Rearrange the words to form sentences with '**nicht**'.

Example: Sie sportlich nicht ist ....*Sie ist nicht sportlich.*..........

a an nicht ziehe Ich mich ....

b Schule wird zur morgen Er gehen nicht ....

c geben jetzt das Geschenk nicht ihr Wir ....

d nicht zur Party Du am Abend gehen sollst ....

6 Rewrite the sentences in the negative using '**nicht**'.
Read the information in English to know which bit to emphasise.

Example Wir fahren nächsten Sommer nach Griechenland. *(We will go next spring.)*

..........*Wir fahren nicht nächsten Sommer nach Griechenland.*..........

a Er hat gestern seinem Bruder eine SMS geschickt. *(He sent one to his sister.)*

....

b Ich werde morgen früh mit einem Freund schnell joggen. *(I will jog slowly.)*

....

c Sie sind letzte Woche zusammen in die Stadt gefahren. *(It was us who went.)*

....

7 Circle either '**aber**' or '**sondern**' to complete the sentences correctly.

a Sie lernen nicht Französisch, **aber** / **sondern** Spanisch.

b Ich hasse Sport, **aber** / **sondern** ich klettere gern.

c Meine Mutter singt nicht nur gut, **aber** / **sondern** spielt auch viele Instrumente.

Separable Verbs & Giving Orders

1 Complete the sentences, using the present tense form of the separable verb in **bold**.

a Ich .... um acht Uhr .... **aufstehen**

b Normalerweise .... er abends .... **ausgehen**

c Am Montag .... meine Großeltern .... **ankommen**

d Immer .... ich viel Geld im Geschäft .... **ausgeben**

e Unsere Stunde .... plötzlich .... **anfangen**

f In meiner Freizeit .... ich gern .... **fernsehen**

g .... Sie sofort damit .... ! **aufhören**

H

h .... Sie bitte Ihre Tasche .... ! **mitnehmen**

2 Rearrange the words to form sentences. There may be more than one possible answer.

Example: halb kommt Flugzeug um das an elf _Das Flugzeug kommt um halb elf an._

a nächste ich zurück Woche komme ....

b fernsehen du morgen wirst ....

c mitgenommen Computer hat seinen er ....

H d hörte auf Regen der ....

3 Translate the sentences below into **German**.

a I want to invite my best friend.

....

b My present arrived on Friday. *(perfect tense)*

....

c We will go if you *(du)* take part.

....

Higher d Did you *(du)* go out last night? *(simple past)*

....

4 Change these sentences into imperatives.

a   Du stellst das Buch hin. ....

b   Ihr geht in die Schule. ....

c   Ihr esst Frühstück. ....

d   Du machst deine Hausaufgaben. ....

e   Sie arbeiten in Ihrem Garten. ....

f   Sie bringen Ihren Hund mit. ....

g   Du besuchst deine Großeltern. ....

h   Ihr glaubt mir. ....

5 Complete these imperative phrases, using the English translation to help you.

a   .... viel Wasser! — *Drink lots of water! (Sie)*

b   .... diese Medikamente! — *Take this medication! (du)*

c   .... nach Hause! — *Go home! (ihr)*

d   .... die Katze mit! — *Bring the cat with you! (ihr)*

e   .... Tennis mit mir! — *Play tennis with me! (du)*

f   .... sich bitte! — *Sit down, please! (Sie)*

g   .... die Frau! — *Ask the woman! (Sie)*

h   .... deinem Bruder! — *Help your brother! (du)*

6 Translate these sentences into **German**.

a   Don't go to the cinema! *(Sie)* ....

b   Bring your sister with you! *(du)* ....

c   Give me a sheet of paper! *(Sie)* ....

d   Don't be late! *(ihr)* ....

e   Work in the kitchen! *(ihr)* ....

f   Take lots of photos! *(du)* ....

Modal Verbs, the Conditional & the Subjunctive

1 Write in the correct present tense form of the following modal verbs, matching the person given.

a wollen — ich ....

f können — wir ....

b mögen — du ....

g müssen — ich ....

c dürfen — er ....

h mögen — ihr ....

d müssen — sie *(sing.)* ....

i wollen — wir ....

e sollen — Sie ....

j dürfen — sie *(pl.)* ....

2 Circle the correct simple past form of the verb to match each person.

a ich musste / mussten / musstet

f Sie wollten / wollte / wolltest

b du solltet / sollten / solltest

g sie *(pl.)* solltest / solltet / sollten

c er konntet / konnte / konntest

h ihr mochte / mochtet / mochten

d sie *(sing.)* mochte / mochtest / mochtet

i wir durften / dürften / durftet

e ich durfte / durften / durftest

j sie *(pl.)* wollten / wolltest / wollte

Higher

3 Translate the sentences below into **German**.

a I am supposed to stay at home, but I want to go with him.

....

b They must be very beautiful.

....

c You *(informal pl.)* can speak German very well.

....

d I had to learn French when I was five.

....

Higher **e** We wanted to write an email, but we didn't have a computer.

....

4 Complete the sentences using '**möcht-**' and the correct ending.

a Ich .... viel Sport treiben, aber ich bin ziemlich faul.

b Du .... Musik hören, aber dein Handy funktioniert nicht mehr.

c Wir .... auf Urlaub fahren, aber wir haben kein Geld dafür.

d Ihr .... gute Noten bekommen, aber ihr arbeitet wenig.

e Chris .... Tennis spielen, aber es gibt keinen Club in der Nähe.

f Sie .... früher ankommen, aber sie können keine Flugtickets kaufen.

5 Translate the sentences below into **English**.

a Ich denke, dass du eine fantastische Anwältin wärst.

....

b Sollten wir zum Abendessen Hähnchen oder Fisch kochen?

....

c Ich würde mit dir in die Stadt fahren, aber ich sollte mehr Geld sparen.

....

d Du hättest einen Hund, aber Tiere gefallen deiner Schwester nicht.

....

6 Translate the sentences below into **German**.

a If I were not so tired, I would go jogging today.

....

b If I were at home, I would eat ice cream.

....

c It would be better if we went to the cinema tomorrow.

....

d If I had more paper, I would write a lot of letters.

....

Higher

Answers

The answers to the translation questions are sample answers only, just to give you an idea of one way to translate them. There may be different ways to translate these sentences that are also correct.

For dictation and translation questions, this symbol (|) shows where to divide the marks. There is 1 mark awarded for the first part of the text, and 1 mark awarded for the second.

Section One — General Stuff

Pages 2-3: Numbers, Times and Dates

1) Holiday in Switzerland — spring
   A wedding — 1st October
2) a) April ist | im Frühling.
   b) Dienstags gehe ich | in den Park.
   c) Es gibt ungefähr | dreißig Häuser.
   d) Am Nachmittag soll ich | meinen Opa anrufen.
   e) Gestern habe ich die Schule | um halb fünf verlassen.
3) a) fifteen minutes
   b) the third street (on the right)
   c) around forty metres
   d) ten euros
4) a) Saturday evening
   b) eighty euros
   c) six months

Pages 4-5: Questions and Being Polite

1) a) Reist
   b) ein
   c) wir
2) a) Wann fährst du | zum Dom?
   b) Willkommen in | meinem Haus.
   c) Ich entschuldige | mich bei ihr.
   d) Ich hätte gern | ein neues Kaninchen.
3) a) from her sister
   b) tomorrow
   c) If she can bring her dog
      If there is something she can eat on the menu
4) a) Sie danken mir | immer herzlich.
   b) Wofür hat sie | das Geld gebraucht?
   c) Was können wir spielen, | ohne ihn zu stören?

Pages 6-7: Opinions

1) a) T
   b) K
   c) N
   d) T
   e) K
3) a) He finds it a bit hard / difficult.
   b) It's boring.
   c) It is / was wonderful.
   d) It was very exciting / thrilling.
4) a) P + N   b) N   c) P   d) P

Section Two — Identity and Relationships with Others

Pages 8-9: About Yourself and My Family & Friends

2) a) Ich habe | keine jüngeren Geschwister.
   b) Er ist | in Norwegen geboren.
   c) Du bist deinem | Bruder sehr ähnlich.
   d) Mein Zwilling wohnt | jetzt in der Schweiz.
4) a) Any two from:
      He had lots of friends at school.
      It was pretty.
      There was lots to do.
   b) His grandma became ill.
   c) It is (actually) better (than his life in Heidelberg).

Pages 10-11: Describing People and Relationships

1) Here are some examples of sentences you could have written:
   Es ist eine Hochzeit.
   Es gibt viele Leute.
   Sie sind am Strand.
   Es gibt zwei Kinder.
   Das Paar scheint glücklich.
3) a) She is his neighbour.
   b) She is (very) funny.
   c) He is annoying/irritating.
4) a) A
   b) C
   c) C

Section Three — Healthy Living and Lifestyle

Pages 12-13: Food and Healthy & Unhealthy Living

2) a) keinen   b) treibt
3) a) B   b) D   c) A
5) a) B   b) A   c) A + B

Pages 14-15: Illnesses and Treatments

1) a) her back
      her head
   b) slept (more)
      drunk (a lot of) water
   c) C
3) a) He has leg pain.
   b) He injured his leg in a football match.
   c) She can bandage his leg.
   d) to relax
   e) medicine

Section Four — Education

Pages 16-17: School Subjects and School Life
2) a) B b) C c) A
4) a) 8.30 am
   b) by train
   c) physics
   d) She could buy tasty snacks.
   e) the gymnasium

Pages 18-19: School Pressures and Difficulties
1) a) D b) A c) F d) C
4) a) N b) F c) P d) P

Section Five — Future Study and Work

Pages 20-21: Education Post-16 and Career Choices
1) a) Ich werde mich | für die Universität entscheiden.
   b) Letztes Jahr hat meine Schwester | eine Lehre begonnen.
3) a) Tove:
   Job — singer
   Quality — creative / musical
   b) Hans:
   Job — director (of a company) / headteacher / principal
   Quality — strong / patient
5) a) N b) P c) F d) F

Theme 1 — Mixed Practice

Pages 22-24: Mixed Practice — Foundation
1) a) E b) D c) B
2) a) Mein Stiefbruder | ist bi(sexuell).
   b) Ab und zu isst | meine Familie Fastfood.
   c) Morgen werde ich | zum Arzt / zur Ärztin gehen.
   d) Letztes Jahr waren | meine Lehrer sehr hilfsbereit.
3) a) 4, B
   b) 2, A
5) a) F b) P c) N
6) a) A b) C c) A

Pages 25-27: Mixed Practice — Both Tiers
1) a) On Mondays I go | to the gym.
   b) The pupil asks | about the homework.
   c) I like my sister, | but my cousin is mean.
   d) In the past he really wanted | to work as a carer.
   e) My parents split up | five years ago.
3) a) Any two from: patient, honest, funny
   b) She doesn't have time for a relationship.
   c) His partner doesn't support his interests.
   d) A
4) a) C b) C
5) a) Mein Vater möchte | heute kochen.
   b) Die Frau sorgt sich oft | um ihre Gesundheit.
   c) Am Sonntag haben wir | zusammen Eis gegessen.
   d) Es ist das Ziel meines Freund(e)s / meiner Freundin, |
   in einer Fabrik zu arbeiten.

Pages 28-31: Mixed Practice — Higher
2) a) Right now she is | preparing for the (job) interview.
   b) I drink no coffee in the evening |
   in order to fall asleep more quickly.
   c) Last month he gave up | alcohol for his health.
   d) When I am older, | I will have lots of tattoos.
   e) As a child, I hardly did sport | because it was tiring.
3) a) A b) C c) C d) B
4) a) they chat almost every day.
   b) his boyfriend often criticises him.
   c) explain his feelings to his boyfriend.
   d) you trust each other.
5) a) Dieses Gericht | ist unglaublich lecker.
   b) Gestern haben sie versprochen, | freundlicher zu sein.
   c) Ich habe eine österreichische Frau | auf der Hochzeit
   kennengelernt.
   d) Obwohl er viel lernt, | musste er sitzenbleiben.
   e) Ich werde eine Lehre machen, | statt an der Universität
   zu studieren.
6) a) A + B b) A

Section Six — Free-time Activities

Pages 32-33: Cinema, TV and Music
2) a) C and D b) A and E
4) a) Z b) Z + M c) M

Pages 34-35: Sport, Going Out and Other Hobbies
1) a) B b) N c) B d) G
3) a) yesterday
   b) by bike
   c) lots of (tasty) food (choices)
   d) noisy / loud people
4) a) I visit the museum because | I find history interesting.
   b) She runs faster than | the other players in the team.
   c) Three years ago he won | a tennis competition.

Section Seven —
Customs, Festivals and Celebrations

Pages 36-37: Customs, Festivals and Celebrations
1) a) A b) C c) B
4) a) about seven weeks before Easter
   b) Cologne
   c) Any two from:
   wear colourful costumes
   wear masks
   play music

Section Eight — Celebrity Culture

Pages 38-39: Favourite Celebrities and Celebrity Life

2) a) Any one from:
   having a comfortable life
   sharing his work with the public
   b) journalists following him
   c) making his fans happy

3) a) Ich lese etwas | über den Sänger.
   b) Der Autor will | viele Preise gewinnen.
   c) Er hat sich | die Kritik angehört.
   d) Der Schauspieler hat eine | gute Beziehung zu seinen Fans.

Theme 2 — Mixed Practice

Pages 40-42: Mixed Practice — Foundation

2) a) Christmas
   goes to church (with his parents)
   b) Eid
   eats traditional food (with her family)

3) a) He receives | a gift.
   b) I want to sing | in a group.
   c) We go jogging, | but he plays video games.
   d) On the train I read | a book or a newspaper.
   e) The famous actress | has won many awards.

5) a) E b) B c) F d) C

6) a) Der / Die Künstler(in) | ist beliebt.
   b) Meine Schwester freut sich | auf den Wettbewerb.
   c) Ich habe meinen Geburtstag | mit meiner Familie gefeiert.
   d) Er möchte seine Freunde | zur Feier einladen.

Pages 43-46: Mixed Practice — Both Tiers

1) a) Ich spiele | gern Fußball.
   b) Mein(e) Lieblingsautor(in) | hat viele Fans.
   c) Nächstes Jahr möchte er | an einem Spiel teilnehmen.
   d) Die Hochzeit hat | im April stattgefunden.
   e) Letzten Monat haben wir viele Museen besucht, |
   um verschiedene Ausstellungen zu sehen.

2) a) E b) B c) F d) C

4) a) Sie ist sportlicher | als ich.
   b) Der Star hat | eine aufregende Karriere.
   c) Zu Weihnachten will ich | viel Kuchen essen.
   d) Als Kind habe ich | Geige gespielt.
   e) Ich möchte die neue Folge | meiner Lieblingsserie gucken.

5) a) (in) July
   b) two hundred
   c) colourful clothes
   d) in a (historic) church

6) a) (somewhat) strange / funny / weird
   b) tired
   c) go to a swimming club
   spend more time with her family

7) a) C b) B c) C d) A

Pages 47-49: Mixed Practice — Higher

2) a) the big meal (on Easter Sunday)
   b) the Christmas markets
   c) money
   d) hides (Easter) eggs for their brother to find

4) a) P b) P + N c) N d) P + N

5) a) In the restaurant | I sat next to my aunt.
   b) She said that | we will watch the fireworks.
   c) I am a big fan of the actress | who played the main part.
   d) New Year's Eve is my favourite celebration | because my
   friends and I always have a good time.
   e) On Sunday I am going to an exhibition | in order to see
   well-known artworks / works of art.

6) a) character, stage
   b) adverts, atmosphere / mood

Section Nine — Travel and Tourism

Pages 50-51: Where to Go, Accommodation and Travel

1) a) N   b) F   c) P   d) F

2) a) F   b) B   c) E

3) a) car
   b) They are often punctual. /
   The view out of the window is beautiful.
   c) There was a lot of traffic (on the way).
   d) It was her first time travelling by boat.
   e) They were often late.

Pages 52-53: What to Do

1) a) N   b) N   c) P + N   d) P

4) a) They were worried about accidents.
   b) went climbing (in the mountains)
   c) speak the local language
   d) go swimming / swim (in the sea)

Section Ten — Media and Technology

Pages 54-55: Technology and The Internet

1) a) they are (very) cheap
   b) (short) videos
   c) play video games
   d) organise activities (with her friends)

2) a) You can now stream | the news on your mobile phone.
   b) Yesterday I bought something | from a secure source.

4) a) P + N b) P c) N

5) a) B   b) C   c) B

Pages 56-57: Social Media

1) a) A   b) B   c) B

3) a) Wir folgen | einem interessanten Blog.
   b) Ich teile Videos | mit meiner Familie.
   c) Sie hat nie | Online-Mobbing erlebt.

Section Eleven — Where People Live

Pages 58-59: The Home

2) kitchen — modern
living room — comfortable
4) a) Our flat | is very clean.
   b) I want to sleep, | but my neighbour is quite noisy.
   c) He recently closed | the window in the bathroom.
   d) Tomorrow I must remember | to take the key with me.
5) a) huge / giant / enormous / massive
   b) She can relax / chill out in the yard.
      She can (easily) reach the nearest forest on foot.
   c) The roof is broken.

Pages 60-61: The Local Area, Directions and Weather

1) a) B   b) C   c) A
2) a) P   b) P + N   c) N
3) a) Her old shoes weren't comfortable anymore.
   b) Any two from:
      The shoes were cheap.
      Every pair fitted her.
      The shop assistants helped her (a lot).

Section Twelve — Environmental and Social Issues

Pages 62-63: The Environment

1) a) C   b) E   c) B
4) a) B and D
   b) C and F

Pages 64-65: Social Issues

1) a) Er
   b) reiche
   c) gestimmt
   d) wird
2) a) being helpful / cooperative
   b) twice per week
   c) Any two from:
      help the elderly
      organise activities
      talk with the elderly
      (help with) the cooking
3) a) food and clothes
   b) give breakfast to school children (every morning)
   c) collects food (at supermarkets)
   d) violence

Theme 3 — Mixed Practice

Pages 66-69: Mixed Practice — Foundation

2) a) B   b) A   c) C
3) Here are some examples of sentences you could have written:
   Eine Touristin sitzt allein.
   Sie hat eine Kamera.
   Sie macht ein Video.
   Sie trägt ein Kleid.
   Es gibt viele Gebäude.
4) a) F   b) N   c) A   d) A   e) N
5) a) großes
   b) die
   c) bin
   d) er
6) a) on the coast
   b) summer
   c) Hotels need their money.
   d) Some tourists throw litter away on the beach.
7) a) She shares | a post.
   b) We always recycle | our old clothes.
   c) My flat has three rooms, | but there is no garden.
   d) At the moment I am unemployed, | so I am looking for a job.
   e) Last year I stayed | in a cheap hotel.

Pages 70-72: Mixed Practice — Both Tiers

1) a) B and C   b) E and F
3) a) C   b) B   c) E
4) a) Mein Handy | ist kaputt.
   b) Gestern habe ich | ein neues Kleid online bestellt.
   c) Züge sind umweltfreundlicher | als Flugzeuge.
   d) Der / Die Wissenschaftler(in) hat uns | vor Klimawandel gewarnt.
5) a) Dieser Ort hat | ein Krankenhaus.
   b) Ich stehe jeden | Tag früh auf.
   c) Die Regierung will | eine neue Anlage bauen.
6) a) B   b) A   c) C   d) A

Pages 73-75: Mixed Practice — Higher

2) a) particularly bad / serious for children
   b) give money to the poor
   c) gave a man twenty euros
   d) (do more to) reduce unemployment
3) a) Klimawandel ist gefährlich | für die Umwelt.
   b) Die Küche ist das | größte Zimmer in unserem Haus.
   c) Wir fahren in die Stadt, | um einkaufen zu gehen.
   d) Ich bin nicht sicher, | ob ich einen Computer kaufen sollte.
   e) Ich reise nie in Europa, | ohne viele Videos aufzunehmen.
4) a) P   b) F   c) N
5) a) to inform people about biological diversity
   b) Any one from:
      Many animals have been in (the highest) danger
      More types of animals are dying out.
   c) Any two from:
      industry
      destruction of forests / deforestation
      climate change

102

Section Thirteen — Nouns, Cases and Linking Words

Pages 76-77: Nouns

1) a) Eier, Tisch
   b) Tennis
   c) Bruder, Krimis
   d) Kleid, Schwester
   e) Cousin, Eis
   f) Moschee, Stadt
   g) Sonne
   h) Sophie, Kuchen
   i) Freund, Auto
   j) Herr Meyer, Spanien
   k) Sportschuhe
   l) Handtasche
2) a) N   b) F   c) M
   d) M   e) N   f) F
   g) F   h) F   i) M
   j) N   k) N
3) a) die Würste
   b) die Lieder
   c) die Rollen
   d) die Zähne
   e) die Kinder
   f) die Cafés
   g) die Tage
   h) die Einladungen
   i) die Stunden
   j) die Brüder
   k) die Häuser
   l) die Betten
4) a) Junge
   b) Menschen
   c) Herren
   d) Jungen
   e) Jungen
   f) Name
5) a) He speaks French very well.
   b) Jogging is a popular activity.
6) a) Deutschen
   b) Kleinen
   c) Freundlichen
   d) Netten
7) a) Sag mir zuerst das Schlimme.
   b) Sie erwartet viel Gutes.
   c) Ich werde etwas Verrücktes tun.

Pages 78-79: Cases and Articles

1) a) Ich
   b) Mein Bruder
   c) Wir
   d) Mein Vater
   e) ich
   f) du
   g) Mein Freund
   h) ihr
   i) Fußball
   j) Meine Mutter, ich
   k) Frankreich
   l) der Vogel
2) a) eine Hose
   b) ein T-Shirt
   c) Das Auto
   d) Spanisch
   e) Kaffee
   f) soziale Medien
   g) eine E-Mail
   h) einen Film
   i) ein Glas Cola
   j) deine Hausaufgaben
   k) mein Handy
   l) Mathe
3) a) accusative
   b) dative
   c) accusative
   d) nominative
   e) dative
   f) accusative
   g) accusative
   h) nominative
   i) nominative
   j) dative
   k) accusative
4) a) Brüdern
   b) Studenten, Problemen
5) a) meines Bruders
   b) meinem Freund
6) a) den
   b) dem
   c) das
   d) Der
   e) den
   f) des
7) a) Die, ein
   b) dem
   c) Das, einen
   d) ein, der
   e) Die, des
8) a) einen, keine
   b) kein, keinen
   c) Keine
   d) einen, kein
   e) des, einer

Answers

Pages 80-81: Pronouns and Word Order

1) a) Er
   b) Sie
   c) Es
   d) Sie
2) a) Sie
   b) ihr
   c) du
   d) Sie
3) a) ihr
   b) mich
   c) ihn
   d) Ihnen
   e) mir
   f) dir
   g) uns, euch
   h) sie
4) a) Jemand hat mich gestern besucht.
   b) Sie hat niemanden im Geschäft gesehen.
5) a) die
   b) das
   c) der
6) a) den
   b) was
   c) die
   d) das
   e) wo
7) a) Wer
   b) wem
   c) Wer
   d) Wem
   e) wen
   f) Wen
8) a) mich
   b) sich, sich
   c) uns
   d) euch, sich
   e) mir
   f) dir
9) The verb should always be the second idea in the sentence.
   For example:
   a) Ich spiele am Freitag Basketball.
   b) Am Samstag spiele ich Tennis.
   c) Ich werde im Juli Frankreich besuchen.
   d) Im August werde ich nach Frankreich reisen.
   e) Ich fahre am Montag mit dem Bus in die Schule.
   f) Am Dienstag fahre ich mit dem Fahrrad in die Schule.

Pages 82-83: Conjunctions and Prepositions

1) a) oder
   b) und
   c) denn
   d) aber
2) a) Ich bleibe zu Hause, wenn das Wetter schlecht ist.
   b) Er fährt in den Urlaub, obwohl er kein Geld hat.
   c) Meine Mutter hat sehr gut gesungen, als sie jünger war.
   d) Sie lernt jeden Abend, weil sie Prüfungen im Mai hat.
   e) Ich studiere Deutsch, damit ich in München arbeiten kann.
3) a) You can eat either chicken or fish.
   b) She likes studying both geography and history.
   c) He plays neither basketball nor football.
4) a) bis
   b) Nach, durch
   c) gegen
   d) von, für
   e) ohne, zur
   f) mit, über
5) a) ins
   b) der
   c) im
   d) den
   e) dem
   f) die
   g) dem
   h) das
   i) den
   j) einer
6) a) Trotz
   b) Während
   c) Wegen
   d) Statt
7) a) Es gibt einen Tisch im Garten und ein Vogel sitzt darauf.
   b) Er ist Verkäufer und arbeitet dazu / außerdem in einem Café.
   c) Beim Kochen höre ich immer Musik.

Section Fourteen — Adjectives and Adverbs

Pages 84-85: Adjectives

1) a) blöd
   b) langweilig
   c) lustig / witzig / komisch
   d) groß

2) a) braune, grünen, weißen
   b) kleinen, großen, schönen
   c) schwarzen, rote, alten
   d) kleinen, leckeren, frische
   e) gelbe, großen, blauen

3) a) schwarzer, roten, schönen
   b) netten, altes, neuen
   c) guten, neuen
   d) besten, lange, kurzen

4) a) zwei rote Autos
   b) wenige heiße Tage
   c) grüne Taschen
   d) einige kleine Hunde

5)

	Masculine	Feminine	Neuter	Plural
Nominative	mein	meine	mein	meine
Accusative	meinen	meine	mein	meine
Dative	meinem	meiner	meinem	meinen
Genitive	meines	meiner	meines	meiner

6) a) Welcher
   b) Diese
   c) welcher
   d) unser
   e) letzte
   f) Dein

7) a) Hast du viel Wasser getrunken?
   b) Ich habe heute wenig Wasser getrunken.

8) a) langsamer
   b) besser
   c) älter
   d) größer
   e) näher

9) a) die schnellste
   b) am traurigsten
   c) am ältesten
   d) das nächste
   e) das bunteste
   f) das höchste

Pages 86-87: Adverbs

1) a) He sings badly. She dances well.
   b) I drive slowly and you talk a lot.
   c) My brother works hard and swims fast.
   d) Normally he is quite / fairly / pretty lazy. Unfortunately he will certainly / definitely come too late.

2) a) schlecht
   b) langsam
   c) schön
   d) wirklich / echt / eigentlich
   e) glücklich
   f) Plötzlich

3) a) Manchmal scheint die Sonne, aber neulich hat es viel geregnet.
   b) Der Zug ist immer spät. Ich hoffe, dass er nächste Woche pünktlich ist.
   c) Hast du schon in diesem Restaurant gegessen? Ich war gestern Abend hier.

4) a) überall
   b) dort
   c) Morgen
   d) irgendwo
   e) mittwochs
   f) hier

5) a) Al speaks louder / more loudly than Eoin.
   b) Rhys dances just as well as Faiz.
   c) Sami doesn't smile as often as / smiles less often than Aled.
   d) Jo likes tennis just as much as Pete.

6) a) langsamer
   b) schlechter
   c) mehr
   d) besser
   e) lieber

7) a) am besten
   b) am liebsten
   c) am schnellsten
   d) am meisten
   e) am schrecklichsten
   f) am öftesten / am häufigsten

Answers

Section Fifteen — Verbs and Tenses

Pages 88-89: Present Tense & More Ways to Use Verbs

1) a) höre
   b) lernen
   c) liebt
   d) sagt
   e) schicken
   f) redet
   g) schlage
   h) bringst
   i) studieren
   j) trinkt
   k) stellen
   l) suchst

2) a) fei(e)re
   b) feiert
   c) wandern
   d) wanderst
   e) sammelt
   f) samm(e)le
   g) lächelt
   h) lächeln

3) a) Riyam spielt Fußball.
   b) Mein Bruder schreibt eine E-Mail.
   c) Mein Vater arbeitet samstags.
   d) Christopher schwimmt heute.
   e) Ich wohne seit fünf Jahren hier.

4) a) bin   d) sind
   b) bist   e) seid
   c) ist   f) sind

5) a) habe   d) haben
   b) hast   e) habt
   c) hat   f) haben

6) a) weiß   d) wissen
   b) weißt   e) wisst
   c) weiß   f) wissen

7) a) isst
   b) fährt
   c) findest
   d) liest

8) a) D
   b) A
   c) D
   d) A
   e) D
   f) A
   g) D
   h) D

9) a) Es regnet heute.
   b) Es gibt drei Gebäude.
   c) Es gefällt mir hier in Berlin.
   d) Es geht mir nicht so gut.

10) a) Man hat das Hähnchen gegessen.
    b) Man hat das Fahrrad gestohlen.

11) a) Er versucht, Spanisch zu lernen.
    b) Wir arbeiten, um Geld zu verdienen.
    c) Ich gehe nie nach draußen, ohne eine Brille zu tragen.
    d) Sie gehen klettern, statt ihre Hausaufgaben zu machen. /
       Sie machen ihre Hausaufgaben, statt klettern zu gehen.

Pages 90-91: Past Tense

1) a) machen, gemacht
   b) glauben, geglaubt
   c) brauchen, gebraucht
   d) kaufen, gekauft
   e) fragen, gefragt
   f) wählen, gewählt
   g) besuchen, besucht
   h) essen, gegessen
   i) arbeiten, gearbeitet
   j) erklären, erklärt
   k) benutzen, benutzt
   l) versuchen, versucht
   m) verlieren, verloren
   n) nehmen, genommen

2) a) bleiben
   b) sein
   c) passieren
   d) folgen
   e) gehen
   f) fliegen
   g) sprechen
   h) finden
   i) bringen
   j) verstehen
   k) spazieren
   l) bezahlen

3) a) Ich bin nach München gefahren.
   b) Er hat einen Kuchen gegessen.
   c) Wir haben ein Museum besucht.
   d) Er ist im Bett geblieben.
   e) Das Flugzeug ist schnell geflogen.
   f) Wann bist du ins Geschäft gekommen?
   g) Wir sind um zwei Uhr angekommen.
   h) Die Katze hat viel Milch getrunken.

4) a) war   d) waren
   b) warst   e) wart
   c) war   f) waren

5) a) hatte   d) hatten
   b) hattest e) hattet
   c) hatte   f) hatten

6) a) machten, störten
   b) kaufte, kaufte
   c) arbeitete, arbeiteten
   d) spieltest, besuchtest
   e) liebten, liebtet
   f) hasste, hassten

7) a) ich kam
   b) er lief
   c) ich half
   d) du sahst
   e) sie dachten
   f) ihr nahmt
   g) ich gab
   h) er schrieb
   i) du wusstest
   j) wir gingen

8) a) Ich fuhr nach Köln und sang in der Kirche.
   b) Wir aßen Fastfood, tranken Cola und sahen fern.

Pages 92-93: Talking about the Future & Negative Forms

1) a) Diesen Sommer gehen wir jeden Tag schwimmen.
   b) Ich kaufe nächstes Jahr ein Haus.
   c) Morgen trinke ich nur Wasser.

2) a) wirst
   b) werdet
   c) wird
   d) werde
   e) werden
   f) werden
   g) wird
   h) Werden

3) a) Nächstes Jahr werde ich viel Sport machen und regelmäßig Tennis spielen.
   b) Nächste Woche wird Andre mit dem Bus in die Stadt fahren.
   c) Diesen Sommer wird es viele gute Filme geben.

4) a) Have you done nothing today?
   b) She never told me the funny story.
   c) He did not go to the coast yesterday.

5) a) Ich ziehe mich nicht an.
   b) Er wird morgen nicht zur Schule gehen.
   c) Wir geben ihr jetzt das Geschenk nicht.
   d) Du sollst am Abend nicht zur Party gehen.

6) a) Er hat gestern nicht seinem Bruder eine SMS geschickt.
   b) Ich werde morgen früh mit einem Freund nicht schnell joggen.
   c) Nicht sie sind letzte Woche zusammen in die Stadt gefahren.

7) a) sondern
   b) aber
   c) sondern

Pages 94-95: Separable Verbs & Giving Orders

1) a) Ich <u>stehe</u> um acht Uhr <u>auf</u>.
   b) Normalerweise <u>geht</u> er abends <u>aus</u>.
   c) Am Montag <u>kommen</u> meine Großeltern <u>an</u>.
   d) Immer <u>gebe</u> ich viel Geld im Geschäft <u>aus</u>.
   e) Unsere Stunde <u>fängt</u> plötzlich <u>an</u>.
   f) In meiner Freizeit <u>sehe</u> ich gern <u>fern</u>.
   g) <u>Hören</u> Sie sofort damit <u>auf</u>!
   h) <u>Nehmen</u> Sie bitte Ihre Tasche <u>mit</u>!

2) Possible answers:
   a) Ich komme nächste Woche zurück.
   b) Du wirst morgen fernsehen.
   c) Er hat seinen Computer mitgenommen.
   d) Der Regen hörte auf.

3) a) Ich will meinen besten Freund / meine beste Freundin einladen.
   b) Mein Geschenk ist am Freitag angekommen.
   c) Wir werden gehen, wenn du teilnimmst.
   d) Gingst du gestern Abend aus?

4) a) Stell(e) das Buch hin!
   b) Geht in die Schule!
   c) Esst Frühstück!
   d) Mach(e) deine Hausaufgaben!
   e) Arbeiten Sie in Ihrem Garten!
   f) Bringen Sie Ihren Hund mit!
   g) Besuch(e) deine Großeltern!
   h) Glaubt mir!

5) a) Trinken Sie
   b) Nimm
   c) Geht / Fahrt
   d) Bringt
   e) Spiel(e)
   f) Setzen Sie
   g) Fragen Sie
   h) Hilf

6) a) Gehen Sie nicht ins Kino!
   b) Bring(e) deine Schwester mit!
   c) Geben Sie mir ein Blatt Papier!
   d) Seid / Kommt nicht spät!
   e) Arbeitet in der Küche!
   f) Mach(e) viele Fotos!

Pages 96-97: Modal Verbs, the Conditional & the Subjunctive

1) a) will
   b) magst
   c) darf
   d) muss
   e) sollen
   f) können
   g) muss
   h) mögt
   i) wollen
   j) dürfen

2) a) musste
   b) solltest
   c) konnte
   d) mochte
   e) durfte
   f) wollten
   g) sollten
   h) mochtet
   i) durften
   j) wollten

3) a) Ich soll zu Hause bleiben, aber ich will mit ihm (mit)gehen.
   b) Sie müssen sehr schön sein.
   c) Ihr könnt sehr gut Deutsch (sprechen).
   d) Ich musste Französisch lernen, als ich fünf war.
   e) Wir wollten eine E-Mail schreiben, aber wir hatten keinen Computer.

4) a) möchte
   b) möchtest
   c) möchten
   d) möchtet
   e) möchte
   f) möchten

5) a) I think that you would be a fantastic lawyer.
   b) Should we cook chicken or fish for our evening meal?
   c) I would go into town with you, but I should save more money.
   d) You would have a dog, but your sister doesn't like animals.

6) a) Wenn ich nicht so müde wäre, würde ich heute joggen (gehen).
   b) Wenn ich zu Hause wäre, würde ich Eis essen.
   c) Es wäre besser, wenn wir morgen ins Kino gehen würden.
   d) Wenn ich mehr Papier hätte, würde ich viele Briefe schreiben.

Foundation Speaking Questions — Mark Scheme

It's very difficult to mark the speaking questions yourself because there isn't one 'right' answer for most questions. To make them easier to mark, record yourself and use a dictionary, or get someone who's really good at German to mark how well you did. Use the mark schemes below to help you, but bear in mind that they're only a rough guide. Ideally, you need a German teacher who knows the AQA mark schemes well to mark it properly.

Role-play (10 marks)

In the Role-play, you'll be marked on how accurately you respond to spoken language.
There are 2 marks available for each of the five tasks in the Role-play (10 marks in total).

Marks	Role-play task
2	You convey your message without ambiguity.
1	You partially convey your message with some ambiguity.
0	None of your message is conveyed.

Reading aloud (15 marks)

The Reading aloud task is divided into two parts. There are 5 marks available for reading
the text aloud, and then 10 marks are available for answering the four compulsory questions.

Marks	Reading the text
5	Your pronunciation may contain minor errors and a few major errors.
4	Your pronunciation contains regular minor and some major errors.
3	Your pronunciation contains frequent minor and major errors.
2	Your pronunciation is rarely accurate.
1	Your pronunciation is very rarely accurate.
0	Does not meet the standard required for 1 mark.

Marks	Responding to the questions
9-10	You answer all questions clearly. At least two answers have an extended response and at least one other is developed well.
7-8	You answer at least three questions clearly. One answer has an extended response and at least one other is developed well.
5-6	You answer at least two questions clearly. One answer is developed well and at least one other is developed minimally.
3-4	You answer at least two questions understandably. One answer is developed minimally.
1-2	You answer at least one question understandably. The answer(s) may be a very limited response.
0	Does not meet the standard required for 1 mark.

Photo card (25 marks)

For the Photo card task, you're marked on three separate criteria. 5 marks are available for your response to the content of the photos on the card, whilst 20 marks are available for the unprepared conversation — 15 marks for 'communication' and 5 marks for 'grammar and vocabulary'.

Marks	Describing the photos
5	You convey quite a lot of information. Information may lack clarity from time to time.
4	You convey some information. Information lacks clarity from time to time.
3	You convey some information. Information lacks clarity from time to time and occasionally messages break down.
2	You convey little information. Messages regularly break down.
1	You convey very little information. Messages regularly break down or the language produced is barely understandable.
0	Does not meet the standard required for 1 mark.

Marks	Unprepared conversation — communication
13-15	You convey quite a lot of information and regularly develop your responses well. Information may lack clarity from time to time.
10-12	You convey some information. You develop some responses well and regularly develop responses minimally. Information lacks clarity from time to time.
7-9	You convey some information and there is regular minimal development of your responses. Information lacks clarity from time to time and occasionally messages break down.
4-6	You convey little information and give limited responses with occasional minimal development. Messages regularly break down.
1-3	You convey very little information with limited responses. Messages regularly break down or hardly anything is said.
0	Does not meet the standard required for 1 mark.

Marks	Unprepared conversation — grammar and vocabulary
5	You use a good variety of vocabulary and structures, but with some repetition. You make frequent minor errors. Some major errors may occur even in basic language.
4	You use some variety of vocabulary and structures, but with regular repetition. You make frequent minor errors and some major errors in most responses to questions.
3	You use a limited variety of vocabulary and structures with regular repetition. You make very frequent minor and frequent major errors in most responses to questions.
2	You use a very limited variety of vocabulary and structures with regular repetition. You make very frequent minor and major errors in nearly all responses to questions.
1	You use hardly any variety of vocabulary and structures. You make minor and major errors in all responses to questions.
0	Does not meet the standard required for 1 mark.

Higher Speaking Questions — Mark Scheme

Role-play (10 marks)

In the Role-play, you'll be marked on how accurately you respond to spoken language. There are 2 marks available for each of the five tasks in the Role-play (10 marks in total). If you are required to give two responses or details in one task, failure to convey an unambiguous message in reply to one of them means that the message is partially conveyed and one mark is awarded.

Marks	Role-play task
2	You convey your message without ambiguity.
1	You partially convey your message with some ambiguity.
0	None of your message is conveyed.

Reading aloud (15 marks)

The Reading aloud task is divided into two parts. There are 5 marks available for reading the text aloud, and then 10 marks are available for answering the four compulsory questions.

Marks	Reading the text
5	Your pronunciation is always or nearly always accurate but you may make an occasional minor error.
4	Your pronunciation contains a few minor errors.
3	Your pronunciation contains some minor errors and very occasional major errors.
2	Your pronunciation contains minor errors and a few major errors.
1	Your pronunciation contains regular minor and some major errors.
0	Does not meet the standard required for 1 mark.

Marks	Responding to the questions
9-10	You answer all questions clearly. At least two answers have an extended response and at least one other is developed well.
7-8	You answer at least three questions clearly. One answer has an extended response and at least one other is developed well.
5-6	You answer at least two questions clearly. One answer is developed well and at least one other is developed minimally.
3-4	You answer at least two questions understandably. One answer is developed minimally.
1-2	You answer at least one question understandably. The answer(s) may be a very limited response.
0	Does not meet the standard required for 1 mark.

Photo card (25 marks)

For the Photo card task, you're marked on three separate criteria. 5 marks are available for your response to the content of the photos on the card, whilst 20 marks are available for the unprepared conversation — 15 marks for 'communication' and 5 marks for 'grammar and vocabulary'.

Marks	Describing the photos
5	You convey a lot of information. Information is always conveyed clearly.
4	You convey a lot of information. Information is nearly always conveyed clearly.
3	You convey quite a lot of information. Information is nearly always conveyed clearly.
2	You convey quite a lot of information. Information may lack clarity from time to time.
1	You convey some information. Information may lack clarity from time to time.
0	Does not meet the standard required for 1 mark.

Marks	Unprepared conversation — communication
13-15	You convey a lot of information with consistent good development and regular extended responses. Information is always or nearly always conveyed clearly.
10-12	You convey a lot of information with consistent good development and some extended responses. Information is conveyed clearly, with occasional lapses.
7-9	You convey quite a lot of information with consistent good development and occasional extended responses. Information is generally conveyed clearly.
4-6	You convey quite a lot of information with regular good development of responses. Information may lack clarity from time to time.
1-3	You convey some information with good development and regular minimal development of responses. Information may lack clarity from time to time.
0	Does not meet the standard required for 1 mark.

Marks	Unprepared conversation — grammar and vocabulary
5	You use a wide variety of vocabulary and structures. You make a few minor errors but few or no major errors when you attempt more complex language.
4	You use a very good variety of vocabulary and structures. You make some minor errors and some major errors when you attempt more complex language.
3	You use a good variety of vocabulary and structures with occasional repetition. You make quite a lot of minor errors and occasional major errors, not only in attempts at more complex language.
2	You use a good variety of vocabulary and structures with some repetition. You make frequent minor errors and some major errors, even with basic language.
1	You use some variety of vocabulary and structures but with regular repetition. You make frequent minor errors and some major errors in most responses to questions.
0	Does not meet the standard required for 1 mark.

Answers

Foundation Writing Questions — Mark Scheme

As with the speaking questions, it's difficult to mark the writing questions yourself because there are no 'right' answers. You ideally need a German teacher who knows the AQA mark schemes to mark your answers properly. Each of the writing tasks has a different mark scheme.

Photo Question (10 marks)

For this question, you're required to write five sentences to describe a photo. There are 2 marks available for each of the five sentences (10 marks in total).

Marks	Communication
2	You convey a relevant message clearly.
1	You convey a relevant message with some ambiguity which causes a delay in communication.
0	Your message is irrelevant or cannot be understood.

10-mark Writing Question

For this question, there are five compulsory bullet points. There are 5 marks available for 'Communication' and 5 marks for 'Grammar and vocabulary'.

Marks	Communication
5	You cover all five bullet points and communicate clearly.
4	You cover at least four bullet points. Your communication is mostly clear with occasional lapses in clarity.
3	You cover at least three bullet points. Your communication is generally clear with several lapses in clarity.
2	You cover at least two bullet points. Your communication is sometimes clear with regular lapses in clarity.
1	You cover at least one bullet point. Your communication is often not clear with many lapses in clarity.
0	Does not meet the standard required for 1 mark.

Marks	Grammar and vocabulary
5	You use a variety of vocabulary and grammatical structures with some minor errors.
4	You use some variety of vocabulary and grammatical structures. You make frequent minor errors with an occasional major error.
3	You attempt to use a variety of vocabulary and grammatical structures. You make frequent minor errors with some major errors.
2	You use limited or repetitive vocabulary and grammatical structures. You make frequent minor errors and a number of major errors.
1	You show little awareness of appropriate vocabulary and grammatical structures. You make errors in the vast majority of sentences.
0	Does not meet the standard required for 1 mark.

15-mark Writing Question

For this question, there are three compulsory bullet points that you must cover — you don't need to cover the bullet points equally. There are 10 marks available for 'Communication' and 5 marks for 'Grammar and vocabulary'.

Marks	Communication
9-10	You cover all three bullet points and communicate clearly. Your ideas are regularly developed and you convey a lot of relevant information.
7-8	You cover all three bullet points and your communication is mostly clear with occasional lapses in clarity. Your ideas are often developed and you convey quite a lot of relevant information.
5-6	You cover at least two bullet points and your communication is generally clear with some lapses in clarity. A few of your ideas may be developed and some relevant information is conveyed.
3-4	You cover at least one bullet point and your communication is sometimes clear with regular lapses in clarity. You convey little relevant information.
1-2	You cover at least one bullet point. Your communication is often not clear and there are very many lapses in clarity. You convey very little relevant information.
0	Does not meet the standard required for 1 mark.

Marks	Grammar and vocabulary
5	You use a good variety of vocabulary with regular attempts at complex language and structures. You make successful references to all three time frames. Errors are mainly minor but you may make some major errors, particularly in complex structures and sentences.
4	You use a variety of vocabulary with some attempts at complex language and structures. You make mainly successful references to at least two different time frames. You make mainly minor errors and some major errors.
3	You use a variety of vocabulary and occasionally attempt complex language and structures. You make references to at least two time frames, although these may not always be successful. You make some major errors and regular minor errors but overall the response is more accurate than inaccurate.
2	You use a limited variety of vocabulary and use mainly simple language with some attempts at longer sentences using appropriate linking words. You may not reference different time frames successfully. You make frequent major and minor errors and your response is generally inaccurate.
1	You use a narrow and/or repetitive range of vocabulary. You use simple language and short sentences that may not be properly constructed. You make no successful references to different time frames. You make frequent major and minor errors and overall your response is highly inaccurate.
0	Does not meet the standard required for 1 mark.

Higher Writing Questions — Mark Scheme

15-mark Writing Question

For this question, there are three compulsory bullet points that you must cover — you don't need to cover the bullet
points equally. There are 10 marks available for 'Communication' and 5 marks for 'Grammar and vocabulary'.

Marks	Communication
9-10	You cover all three bullet points and communicate clearly. Your ideas are developed and you convey a lot of information.
7-8	You cover all three bullet points and mostly communicate clearly. Your ideas are often developed and you convey quite a lot of information.
5-6	You cover at least two bullet points and generally communicate clearly. You develop a few ideas and convey some information.
3-4	You cover at least one bullet point and sometimes communicate clearly. You convey little information.
1-2	You cover at least one bullet point. Your communication is often unclear and you convey very little information.
0	Does not meet the standard required for 1 mark.

Marks	Grammar and vocabulary
5	You use a good variety of vocabulary with complex language and structures. You use all three time frames and any errors are mainly minor.
4	You use a variety of vocabulary and attempt to use complex language and structures. You use at least two time frames and errors are mainly minor.
3	You use some variety of vocabulary and occasionally attempt complex language and structures. You try to use at least two time frames. There are regular minor errors and may be some major errors.
2	You use a limited variety of vocabulary and use mainly simple language. You might fail to use different time frames and make regular errors.
1	Your vocabulary is narrow and/or repetitive. You use simple language and structures. You fail to use different time frames and make frequent errors.
0	Does not meet the standard required for 1 mark.

25-mark Writing Question

For this question, there are two compulsory bullet points that you must cover — you don't need to cover the bullet points equally.
There are 15 marks available for 'Communication', 5 marks for 'Range of language' and 5 marks for 'Accuracy of language'.

Marks	Communication
13-15	You convey a lot of information with very few or no lapses in clarity. Your ideas are regularly developed.
10-12	You convey quite a lot of information, and communication is mostly clear with occasional lapses in clarity. Your ideas are often developed.
7-9	You convey an adequate amount of information, and communication is usually clear with some lapses in clarity. A few of your ideas may be developed.
4-6	You convey some information, but communication is sometimes unclear with regular lapses in clarity. There is only a little development of your ideas.
1-3	You convey a limited amount of information, and communication is unclear with frequent lapses in clarity. There is very limited development of ideas.
0	Does not meet the standard required for 1 mark.

Marks	Range of language
5	You use a very good variety of appropriate vocabulary and grammatical structures with regular successful attempts at complex language.
4	You use a good variety of appropriate vocabulary and grammatical structures with regular, generally successful attempts at complex language.
3	You use some variety of appropriate vocabulary and grammatical structures with occasional, sometimes successful attempts at complex language.
2	You use a limited variety of vocabulary and grammatical structures. You often use short and simple structures but also regularly use longer sentences.
1	You use a very limited variety of appropriate vocabulary. You mainly use short and simple structures.
0	Does not meet the standard required for 1 mark.

Marks	Accuracy of language
5	Your response is usually accurate, with occasional errors in attempts at more complex structures. Your verb and tense formations are secure.
4	Your response is generally accurate, with several errors in attempts at more complex structures. Your verb and tense formations are generally correct.
3	Your response is reasonably accurate, with errors in both simple and complex structures. Your verb and tense formations are sometimes correct.
2	Your response is more inaccurate than accurate. There are frequent errors. Your verb and tense formations are often incorrect.
1	Your response is mostly inaccurate and there are errors in all sentences. Your verb and tense formations are nearly always incorrect.
0	Does not meet the standard required for 1 mark.

Listening Transcripts

You can find printable versions of the Listening and Speaking transcripts on the CGP RevisionHub — go to cgpbooks.co.uk/haus.

Section One — General Stuff

Listening Track 1 — p.2

1) **M1:** Ich habe am Freitag Geburtstag, und im Frühling fahre ich in Urlaub in die Schweiz. Am ersten Oktober gehe ich zu einer Hochzeit.

Listening Track 2 — p.3

4a) **F1:** Am Samstagabend gehe ich zu einem Konzert. Ich werde Nina Callmann sehen, die so schön singt.

4b) **F1:** Ich freue mich darauf, aber das Ticket hat achtzig Euro gekostet. Es war etwas teuer, allerdings denke ich, dass es das wert sein wird.

4c) **F1:** Ich musste sechs Monate lang Geld sparen, um mein Ticket zu kaufen. Ich durfte in letzter Zeit nicht so viel online kaufen.

Listening Track 3 — p.4

2a) **M2:** Wann fährst du | zum Dom?

2b) **F2:** Willkommen in | meinem Haus.

2c) **F1:** Ich entschuldige | mich bei ihr.

2d) **M1:** Ich hätte gern | ein neues Kaninchen.

Listening Track 4 — p.7

3a) **F2:** Hallo Rory, hier ist Priya.

M2: Hallo Priya, was ist los?

F2: Möchtest du am Wochenende etwas zusammen machen? Vielleicht können wir zusammen Tennis spielen.

M2: Es tut mir leid, aber ich habe keine Lust auf Tennis, weil ich es ein bisschen schwierig finde.

3b) **M2:** Ich gehe lieber schwimmen. Das ist entspannend. Kommst du mit?

F2: Ich bin mir nicht sicher. Schwimmen ist mir langweilig. Meiner Meinung nach sollen wir etwas draußen an der frischen Luft machen. Ich gehe sehr gern wandern.

M2: Toll! Wandern ist eine gute Idee.

3c) **M2:** Möchtest du auch danach etwas tun?

F2: Ja, warum nicht? Der neue Film von Klaus Klauter läuft im Kino. Meine Schwester hat den Film schon gesehen und meint, dass er wunderbar ist.

3d) **M2:** Der letzte Film von ihm war sehr spannend.

F2: Toll. Ich freue mich schon darauf!

Section Two — Identity and Relationships with Others

Listening Track 5 — p.8

2a) **M2:** Ich habe | keine jüngeren Geschwister.

2b) **F2:** Er ist | in Norwegen geboren.

2c) **M2:** Du bist | deinem Bruder | sehr ähnlich.

2d) **F2:** Mein Zwilling | wohnt jetzt | in der Schweiz.

Listening Track 6 — p.11

3a) **M1:** Ich habe eine kleine Familie. Ich wohne mit meiner Mutter und meinem Bruder zusammen. Ich komme gut mit ihnen aus, aber mein Lieblingsmensch ist meine Tante. Ich sehe sie oft, weil sie unsere Nachbarin ist.

3b) **M1:** Ich besuche sie jeden Tag. Wenn wir zusammen sind, lachen wir viel. Meine Freunde denken, dass sie sehr lustig ist.

3c) **M1:** Es gibt nur ein Problem, wenn ich meine Tante besuche. Leider verstehe ich mich mit meinem Cousin nicht gut. Ich finde ihn ärgerlich.

Section Three — Healthy Living and Lifestyle

Listening Track 7 — p.12

3a) **F1:** Ich bin Elif. Man soll, wenn möglich, Rad fahren und nicht mit dem Auto fahren. Was denkst du, Julian?

3b) **M2:** Genau! Ich will gesund sein, also esse ich jeden Tag Obst. Und wie bleibst du in Form, Sofie?

3c) **F2:** Ab und zu gehe ich ins Fitness-Studio. Ich bewege mich gern und ich will stark werden.

Listening Track 8 — p.15

3a) **F2:** Guten Tag, Herr Hoffmann. Wie kann ich Ihnen helfen?

M1: Hallo. Ich bin heute gekommen, weil ich Schmerzen im Bein habe.

3b) **F2:** Kennen Sie den Grund dafür?

M1: Ich habe letzte Woche Fußball gespielt. Ich habe mein Bein im Spiel verletzt.

3c) **F2:** Ich kann heute das Bein verbinden, aber Sie müssen morgen ins Krankenhaus gehen. Dort kann man es besser untersuchen. Können Sie das machen?

3d) **M1:** Ja, natürlich. Was soll ich inzwischen tun?

F2: Ich würde empfehlen, dass Sie sich entspannen. Wenn Sie viel stehen, könnten die Schmerzen schlimmer werden.

3e) **M1:** Vielen Dank für Ihre Hilfe.

F2: Kein Problem. Bevor Sie nach Hause gehen, werde ich Ihnen Medikamente geben, um die Schmerzen zu reduzieren.

Section Four — Education

Listening Track 9 — p.17

4a) **F1:** Hallo! Ich bin auf dem Weg zur Schule. Für mich fängt der Schultag um halb neun an.

4b) **F1:** Heute fahre ich mit dem Bus. Normalerweise nehme ich den Zug, aber es gibt Probleme auf der Bahnlinie.

4c) **F1:** Meine erste Stunde ist Physik und danach habe ich Theater.

4d) **F1:** Früher bin ich in der Pause in die Kantine gegangen. Die Kantine hat mir gefallen, weil man dort leckere Imbisse kaufen konnte.

4e) **F1:** Jedoch habe ich jetzt keine Zeit dafür, weil ich einen Kurs habe, der in der Turnhalle stattfindet.

Listening Track 10 — p.19

4a) **M2:** Guten Morgen, Yuki. Wie findest du die Schule?

F2: Der Unterricht gefällt mir nicht, denn es gibt zu viele Schüler in der Klasse. Deswegen ist es ganz schwer, den Lehrer zu hören. Mika, wie findest du die Schule?

4b) **M2:** Ich fühle mich in der Schule unter Druck. Nächstes Jahr werden wir Prüfungen machen. Ich muss mich darauf vorbereiten, wenn ich die Prüfungen bestehen will. Was für Herausforderungen hast du in der Schule, Hanna?

4c) **F1:** Früher war ich das Opfer von Mobbing, aber meine Lieblingslehrerin hat mich unterstützt, als ich ihr davon erzählt habe. Glücklicherweise hat sich die Situation sofort verbessert. Jonas, wie findest du die Schule?

4d) **M1:** Die Möglichkeiten sind super. Zum Beispiel habe ich letzten Monat einen Austausch gemacht. Es war absolut fantastisch, weil ich so viel gelernt habe.

112

Section Five — Future Study and Work

Listening Track 11 — p.20

1a) **M1:** Ich werde mich | für die Universität | entscheiden.

1b) **F2:** Letztes Jahr | hat meine Schwester | eine Lehre begonnen.

Listening Track 12 — p.20

3a) **F1:** Ich will Sängerin werden. Man kann mit einer weiteren Ausbildung besser singen. Es ist aber wichtig, dass Sänger kreativ und musikalisch sind.

3b) **M1:** Mein Bruder ist Verkäufer und muss vielen Kunden helfen, aber ich möchte das nicht machen. Ich möchte Direktor werden. Dafür muss ich stark aber auch geduldig sein.

Theme 1 — Mixed Practice

Listening Track 13 — p.23

3) **F1:** Ich habe neulich den Stundenplan bekommen. Ich freue mich auf Montags, denn um Viertel nach elf habe ich mein Lieblingsfach, Kunst. Jedoch habe ich zuerst Erdkunde. Dieses Fach beginnt um neun Uhr. Ich finde die Themen sehr interessant.

Listening Track 14 — p.24

5a) **M2:** Bald werde ich eine neue Stelle als Betreuer anfangen.

5b) **M2:** Früher habe ich als Verkäufer gearbeitet, als ich an der Universität war.

5c) **M2:** Im Moment arbeite ich als Lehrer in einer wunderbaren Schule.

Listening Track 15 — p.27

4) **F2:** Wir haben montags und dienstags Sport. Das ist genug, glaube ich. Ich finde Sprachen viel schwerer als Mathe. Ich mag besonders Mathe und ich hasse Französisch.

Listening Track 16 — p.30

4a) **M2:** Seit zwei Jahren bin ich mit meinem Freund zusammen. Wir unterhalten uns fast jeden Tag, und deswegen haben wir eine enge Beziehung.

4b) **M2:** Er hat viele Eigenschaften, die ich liebe. Zum Beispiel ist er super frech und das bringt mich zum Lachen. Dagegen kritisiert er mich häufig, was ich total hasse.

4c) **F1:** Es tut mir leid, Bastian. Das klingt schwierig. Ich bin der Meinung, dass dein Freund sich wie ein Kind verhält. An deiner Stelle würde ich ihm deine Gefühle erklären. Er sollte auf dich hören, wenn er dich liebt.

4d) **F1:** Danach wird er dich hoffentlich besser verstehen. In einer Beziehung muss man sich gegenseitig vertrauen. Für mich ist das das Wichtigste. Wie kannst du das machen, wenn dein Freund dich nur kritisiert?

Listening Track 17 — p.31

6a) **M2:** Als Kind habe ich gute Noten in Chemie und Physik bekommen. Wegen dieser Noten haben meine Eltern gedacht, dass ich Wissenschaftler werden sollte. Trotzdem war es immer mein eigener Traum, eine Karriere als Anwalt zu haben. Dieser Beruf scheint mir immer noch sehr interessant.

6b) **M2:** Es kann ganz schwierig sein, den perfekten Beruf zu finden. Ich will kein hohes Gehalt, wenn die Arbeit mich gar nicht interessiert. Mir ist eine starke Beziehung zu den anderen Arbeitnehmern und zu den Arbeitgebern viel wichtiger. Deshalb wäre eine tolle Arbeitskultur notwendig für mich.

Section Six — Free-time Activities

Listening Track 18 — p.32

2a) **M2:** Ich finde diesen Film echt interessant. In diesem Film geht es um komplizierte und wichtige Themen, obwohl es eine Komödie ist. Die Schauspieler sind auch fantastisch. Meiner Meinung nach sollten alle diesen Film ansehen.

2b) **F2:** Der Film gefällt mir sehr. Es gab spannende Ereignisse im Film, die mich völlig überrascht haben. Außerdem war die Landschaft schön, denn man hat den Film in den Bergen gedreht. Ich möchte mir den Film nochmal ansehen.

Listening Track 19 — p.35

3a) **M2:** Ich bin gestern zu einem neuen Restaurant im Stadtzentrum gegangen.

3b) **M2:** Ich bin zum Restaurant mit dem Fahrrad gefahren, weil mein Auto kaputt ist.

3c) **M2:** Es war ein schöner Abend. Die Speisekarte war toll. Man konnte viel leckeres Essen bestellen. Ich habe auch das Essen schnell bekommen.

3d) **M2:** Der Abend war fast perfekt, aber die Leute an einem anderen Tisch waren sehr laut. Ich habe das ärgerlich gefunden.

Section Seven — Customs, Festivals and Celebrations

Listening Track 20 — p.36

1a) **F1:** Meine Tante hat neulich geheiratet. Die Hochzeit hat im Frühling, eine kurze Zeit nach dem Geburtstag von meiner Tante, stattgefunden.

1b) **F1:** Die Hochzeit war eine große Feier. Meine Tante hat meine ganze Familie eingeladen. Es gab ein leckeres Essen und einen großen Kuchen.

1c) **F1:** Das Paar hat viele schöne Geschenke bekommen. Nachdem wir viel getanzt haben, haben wir am Ende der Nacht ihr und ihrer neuen Frau viel Glück gewünscht.

Section Eight — Celebrity Culture

Listening Track 21 — p.39

3a) **M1:** Ich lese etwas | über den Sänger.

3b) **F1:** Der Autor will | viele Preise | gewinnen.

3c) **M2:** Er hat sich | die Kritik | angehört.

3d) **F2:** Der Schauspieler hat | eine gute Beziehung | zu seinen Fans.

Theme 2 — Mixed Practice

Listening Track 22 — p.40

2a) **M2:** Am ersten Weihnachtstag gehe ich mit meinen Eltern in die Kirche. Dieses Jahr hat mein Cousin eine große Silvesterfeier, aber ich werde nichts machen.

2b) **F1:** Meine beste Freundin feiert Ostern, weil sie Christin ist. Ich feiere jedoch Eid und zu diesem Fest esse ich ein traditionelles Essen mit meiner Familie.

Listening Track 23 — p.43

2a) **M1:** Als bekannter Schauspieler sehen mich viele Menschen an. Also muss ich immer gut aussehen, und das ist etwas ärgerlich.

2b) **F1:** Viele Zuschauer kommen zu meinen Konzerten. Es macht mich glücklich, wenn sie zu meinen Liedern tanzen.

2c) **M2:** Ich liebe meine Fans, aber sie wollen oft Fotos mit mir. Ich finde das manchmal schwierig, wenn ich ausgehe.

2d) **F2:** Ich nehme an vielen Sportwettbewerben auf der ganzen Welt teil. In andere Länder reisen ist toll. Es kann wirklich anstrengend sein, aber es macht viel Spaß.

Listening Track 24 — p.44

4a) **F2:** Sie ist sportlicher | als ich.

4b) **M2:** Der Star hat | eine aufregende Karriere.

4c) **F2:** Zu Weihnachten will ich | viel Kuchen essen.

4d) **M2:** Als Kind habe ich | Geige gespielt.

4e) **F2:** Ich möchte | die neue Folge | meiner Lieblingsserie gucken.

Listening Track 25 — p.45

5a) **M1:** Im Moment plane ich eine Hochzeit, die im Juli ist. Das ist sehr bald, oder?

5b) **M1:** Es wird eine große Feier geben. Das Paar hat schon zweihundert Gäste eingeladen.

5c) **M1:** Sie wollen, dass die Gäste nur bunte Kleidung tragen. Meiner Meinung nach ist das eine wunderbare Idee.

5d) **M1:** Die Hochzeit wird in einer historischen Kirche stattfinden und ich habe viele Lichter dafür gekauft. Sie werden fantastisch aussehen.

Listening Track 26 — p.47

2a) **F1:** Ich bin Paula. Ich mag Ostern, denn jedes Jahr gehe ich mit meiner Familie in die Kirche und ich treffe meine Freunde. Am besten mag ich aber das große Essen, das am Ostersonntag stattfindet.

2b) **M1:** Ich heiße Julian. Ich werde Weihnachten dieses Jahr in Wien feiern, weil mein Vater dort Cousins hat. Ich interessiere mich für die österreichischen Weihnachtstraditionen aber am meisten freue ich mich auf die Weihnachtsmärkte.

2c) **F2:** Mein Name ist Samira. Meine Familie und ich feiern Eid zusammen. Das Hauptereignis ist ein großes Essen mit traditionellen Gerichten. Dazu schenken wir den Kindern in der Familie Geld.

2d) **M2:** Ich bin Ben. Ich finde, dass Ostern eine schöne Tradition ist, da ich viel Zeit mit meiner Familie verbringen kann. Zum Beispiel verstecke ich mit meiner Schwester Ostereier, damit unser kleiner Bruder sie finden kann.

Listening Track 27 — p.49

6a) **F1:** Morgen fahre ich in die Stadt, weil ich als Geburtstagsgeschenk Karten für ein Theaterstück bekommen habe. Es wird ein super Abend sein. Am meisten freue ich mich darauf, meinen Lieblingscharakter auf der Bühne zu sehen.

6b) **M1:** Am Samstag gehe ich ins Kino, um einen neuen Film anzuschauen. Der Film soll wirklich spannend sein. Leider finde ich die Werbungen absolut schrecklich, dagegen ist die Stimmung immer ganz besonders.

Section Nine — Travel and Tourism

Listening Track 28 — p.50

2a) **F2:** Ich bin in einer Wohnung im Wald geblieben. Leider war es schrecklich, weil die Zimmer sehr schmutzig waren.

2b) **M1:** Ich bin an der Küste geblieben. Wir hatten ein schönes Zimmer und das Hotel war nicht teuer, aber die anderen Gäste waren sehr laut.

2c) **M2:** Das Restaurant in unserem Hotel war sehr nett. Leider haben wir nicht gut geschlafen, da das Bett nicht bequem war.

Listening Track 29 — p.51

3a) **F1:** Hallo Martin! Wie war deine Reise nach Spanien?
   M1: Es war okay. Ich bin zuerst mit meinem Auto zum Flughafen gefahren. Der Flug hat dann drei Stunden gedauert.

3b) **F1:** Fliegst du gern?
   M1: Ja, normalerweise. Flugzeuge sind oft pünktlich und der Blick aus dem Fenster ist schön. Aber diesmal hatte ich schlechte Laune.

3c) **F1:** Warum? Ist etwas passiert?
   M1: Ja. Ich bin spät am Flughafen angekommen, denn es gab unterwegs viel Verkehr. Deshalb hat die Fahrt zwei Stunden gedauert. Das ist nicht normal!
   F1: Ach, schade!

3d) **M1:** Wie war deine Reise, Frida?
   F1: Meine Reise war meistens gut, aber es war so lang. Ich bin zuerst mit dem Boot nach Frankreich gereist. Es war eine besondere Reise, weil ich noch nie mit diesem Verkehrsmittel gereist bin.

3e) **M1:** Wie bist du gereist, als du in Frankreich angekommen bist?
   F1: Als ich in der Stadt angekommen bin, bin ich mit der Straßenbahn gefahren. Das hat mir nicht gefallen, weil die Straßenbahnen oft spät waren. Deshalb war ich oft nicht pünktlich zu den Ausflügen.

Section Ten — Media and Technology

Listening Track 30 — p.54

1a) **M2:** Ich heiße Dimitri. Ich lade oft Apps auf mein Handy herunter. Das ist fantastisch, weil sie sehr billig sind.

1b) **F1:** Ich bin Asli. Es gefällt mir, wenn meine Freundinnen mir kurze Videos schicken. Dann können wir in Kontakt bleiben.

1c) **M1:** Mein Name ist Benedikt. Nach einem langen Schultag spiele ich auf meinem Laptop Videospiele. Das mache ich jeden Abend und es kann manchmal Stunden dauern.

1d) **F2:** Ich heiße Sümeyye. Auf meinem Handy organisiere ich Aktivitäten mit meinen Freunden. Das ist total praktisch. Ich schreibe schnell eine SMS und sofort treffen wir uns.

Listening Track 31 — p.55

5a) **F2:** Meine Oma hat nicht so viel Ahnung von Technik. Deshalb hat sie neulich einen Kurs gemacht, damit sie das Internet gut benutzen kann. Jetzt kann sie uns über Video anrufen.

5b) **F2:** Da meine Oma viele Freunde im Ausland hat, will sie mehr lernen. Als Nächstes möchte sie soziale Medien verwenden. Sie möchte mit ihren Freunden in Kontakt bleiben und auf ihre Fotos online reagieren.

5c) **F2:** Am Anfang hat es meinen Bruder sehr überrascht, als er vom Kurs meiner Oma gehört hat. Aber er ist stolz auf sie, dass sie so modern ist und sich für Technologie interessiert.

Listening Track 32 — p.57

3a) **M1:** Wir folgen | einem interessanten Blog.

3b) **F1:** Ich teile Videos | mit meiner Familie.

3c) **M2:** Sie hat nie | Online-Mobbing erlebt.

Section Eleven — Where People Live

Listening Track 33 — p.58

2) **M1:** Willkommen in meinem Haus! Sie können die Schuhe hier im Gang lassen. Im Gang ist es ziemlich eng, also zeige ich Ihnen jetzt die Küche. Die Küche ist modern, finden Sie nicht? Ich liebe sie sehr. Und hier haben wir das bequeme Wohnzimmer. Sie können hier warten — möchten Sie einen Kaffee?

Listening Track 34 — p.59

5a) **F2:** Seit zwei Jahren wohnen meine Familie und ich in der Schweiz. Wir wohnen heute in einem riesigen Bauernhaus in den Bergen und wir haben keine Nachbarn.

5b) **F2:** Ich finde es angenehm, mich im Hof zu entspannen. Es ist auch super, dass ich den nächsten Wald leicht zu Fuß erreichen kann.

5c) **F2:** Es gibt allerdings ein ernstes Problem mit dem Haus. Das Dach ist im Moment wegen eines starken Winds kaputt. Die ganze Situation ist total verrückt.

Listening Track 35 — p.60

2a) **M2:** In dieser Stadt findet man einen tollen Markt. Man kann dort viel leckeres Essen kaufen.

2b) **M2:** In der Hauptstraße gibt es auch schöne Kleidungsgeschäfte, aber sie sind sehr teuer.

2c) **M2:** Es gibt auch einen Park. Er gefällt mir nicht, weil oft überall Müll liegt.

Section Twelve — Environmental and Social Issues

Listening Track 36 — p.63

4a) **M1:** Obwohl die Anzahl von grünen Energiequellen steigt, gibt es noch viele Kraftwerke, die Schadstoffe produzieren. Viele Fahrzeuge verschmutzen auch die Luft und sie sind gefährlich für die Natur und die Menschen. Man kann Firmen wählen, die grüne Energie verwenden, um eine positive Veränderung zu machen. Dazu kann man mehr mit Elektroautos fahren.

4b) **F1:** In einigen Gegenden gibt es auch Probleme mit schmutzigen Flüssen, die gefährlich für Fische und andere Tiere sind. Man kann Müll an den Flüssen sammeln. Dazu sollen Unternehmen aufhören, die Flüsse zu verschmutzen.

Listening Track 37 — p.65

3a) **F2:** Hallo, Joel. Die Kosten für notwendige Dinge zum Leben sind so hoch. In unserer Gegend können viele Familien zum Beispiel nicht für Essen und Kleidung zahlen.

3b) **F2:** Einige Schulen wollen helfen und sie geben den Schulkindern jeden Morgen Frühstück.

3c) **M1:** Ja, das ist schade, Lena. Jedoch haben Schulen nicht immer viel Geld. Ich helfe bei einer Freiwilligengruppe, die Essen in Supermärkten sammelt. Jede Woche geben wir es Leuten, die es wirklich brauchen.

3d) **M1:** Leider gibt es auch andere Probleme in unserer Gegend. Leute haben zum Beispiel Angst, weil es auf den Straßen viel Gewalt gibt.

Theme 3 — Mixed Practice

Listening Track 38 — p.66

2a) **F2:** Leider gibt es am Montag keine Sonne mehr. In vielen Regionen wird es den ganzen Tag regnen.

2b) **F2:** Es wird wärmer im Osten als im Westen sein. Im Süden wird es sehr kalt sein.

2c) **F2:** Am Dienstag sollen die Temperaturen aber überall auf fünfundzwanzig Grad steigen.

Listening Track 39 — p.68

6a) **F1:** Ich wohne in einer kleinen Stadt an der Küste. Mein Haus gefällt mir bestimmt, weil es so süß ist.

6b) **F1:** Normalerweise ist die Stadt ganz ruhig, besonders im Winter. Jedoch ist sie im Sommer sehr beliebt bei Touristen.

6c) **F1:** Touristen sind wichtig für unsere Stadt. Zum Beispiel gibt es viele Hotels, die das Geld von Touristen brauchen.

6d) **F1:** Dagegen gibt es auch Nachteile. Einige Touristen werfen Müll am Strand weg. Jedes Jahr gibt es das gleiche Problem und wir haben genug davon.

Listening Track 40 — p.70

1a) **F1:** Ich mache viele Aktivitäten mit einer Umweltschutzgruppe und ich teile Fotos davon auf sozialen Medien. Ich nehme an einem Lauf teil, denn ich will Geld für die Gruppe sammeln.

1b) **M2:** Jeden Monat sammele ich Müll mit meinen Freunden im Wald. Mittwochs gehe ich auch für meine alten Nachbarn einkaufen.

Listening Track 41 — p.71

5a) **F2:** Dieser Ort hat | ein Krankenhaus.

5b) **M1:** Ich stehe | jeden Tag | früh auf.

5c) **F2:** Die Regierung | will eine neue | Anlage bauen.

Listening Track 42 — p.73

2a) **F2:** Das größte Problem in unserer Gesellschaft heute ist der Hunger, denke ich. Was meinst du, Max?
M2: Ich teile deine Meinung, Lola. Der Hunger hat einen besonders schlimmen Effekt auf Kinder.

2b) **F2:** Aber wie kann man dieses Problem lösen?
M2: Die deutsche Bevölkerung kann dabei helfen. Sie sollte den Armen Geld geben.

2c) **F2:** Vielleicht, aber das würde nur für kurze Zeit helfen. Zum Beispiel habe ich letzte Woche einem Mann zwanzig Euro gegeben, aber ich kann mir das nicht jede Woche leisten.

2d) **M2:** Ich verstehe, was du meinst. Die Regierung muss unbedingt langfristig helfen. Sie sollte mehr tun, um Arbeitslosigkeit zu reduzieren.
F2: Das stimmt.

Listening Track 43 — p.74

4) **F1:** Hallo, Jonas. Hast du das neue Online-Videospiel von Studio Eiermann gekauft?
M2: Nein, eigentlich spiele ich keine Videospiele mehr, weil ich danach süchtig war. Und du, Livia? Du wolltest Posts für einen Blog schreiben, oder?
F1: Leider habe ich keinen Fortschritt gemacht, denn ich habe keine Zeit dafür. Jedoch möchte ich bald damit anfangen. Sabri, wie benutzt du das Internet?
M1: Früher musste man jeden Tag eine Zeitung im Geschäft kaufen, aber jetzt sind alle Artikel online. Das ist eine günstige Weise, mich über wichtige Ereignisse in der Welt zu informieren.

Speaking Transcripts

You can find printable versions of the Listening and Speaking transcripts on the CGP RevisionHub — go to cgpbooks.co.uk/haus.

Section Two — Identity and Relationships with Others

Speaking Track 1 — Role-play — p.10

Intro: Du sprichst mit deinem deutschen Freund / deiner deutschen Freundin. Ich bin dein Freund / deine Freundin.
1) Wie sieht dein bester Freund oder deine beste Freundin aus?
2) Warum magst du deinen besten Freund oder deine beste Freundin?
3) Mit wem verstehst du dich gut in deiner Familie?
4) Möchtest du in der Zukunft heiraten? Warum? / Warum nicht?
5) The student will now ask the teacher a question. The teacher should answer.

Section Three — Healthy Living and Lifestyle

Speaking Track 2 — Reading aloud — p.12

Intro: Lies mir den Text vor.
1a) Was isst du normalerweise zum Frühstück?
1b) Wie kann man mehr Energie im Alltagsleben haben?
1c) Wie findest du Sport?
1d) Was denkst du über Alkohol?

Speaking Track 3 — Photo card — p.15

Intro: Sag mir etwas über die Fotos.
4a) Sag mir etwas über eine Zeit, als du krank warst.
4b) Wie findest du Krankenhäuser?
4c) Denkst du, dass Bewegung wichtig ist? Warum? / Warum nicht?
4d) Was sollte man vermeiden, um seine Gesundheit zu schützen?

Section Four — Education

Speaking Track 4 — Reading aloud — p.16

Intro: Lies mir den Text vor.
1a) Kannst du mir deinen Schulalltag beschreiben?
1b) Wie findest du Hausaufgaben?
1c) Was denkst du über deine Lehrer?
1d) Was machst du normalerweise in der Pause?

Speaking Track 5 — Role-play — p.19

Intro: Du sprichst mit deinem deutschen Freund / deiner deutschen Freundin. Ich bin dein Freund / deine Freundin.
1) Was trägst du in der Schule?
2) Wie oft hast du Klassenarbeiten?
3) Kannst du mir ein Problem in deiner Schule beschreiben?
4) Was denkst du über Prüfungen?
5) The student will now ask the teacher a question. The teacher should answer.

Section Five — Future Study and Work

Speaking Track 6 — Role-play — p.21

Intro: Du sprichst mit deinem Freund / deiner Freundin aus der Schweiz. Ich bin dein Freund / deine Freundin.
1) Was ist dein Traumberuf?
2) Was wirst du nach deinen Prüfungen machen?
3) Was denkst du von Lehren?
4) Möchtest du auf die Uni gehen? Warum? / Warum nicht?
5) The student will now ask the teacher a question. The teacher should answer.

Theme 1 — Mixed Practice

Speaking Track 7 — Photo card — p.23

Intro: Sag mir etwas über die Fotos.
4a) Ist es dir wichtig, dass du gesundes Essen wählst? Warum?
4b) Welche Aktivität hast du neulich gemacht?
4c) Treibst du gern Sport in der Schule? Warum? / Warum nicht?
4d) Bewegst du dich lieber mit anderen Menschen oder allein? Warum?

Speaking Track 8 — Reading aloud — p.31

Intro: Lies mir den Text vor.
7a) Was sind die negativen Aspekte von Zigaretten?
7b) Was sollte man tun, um gesünder zu leben?
7c) Was würdest du tun, wenn du dich krank fühlen würdest?
7d) Ist die Ernährung das Wichtigste, um in Form zu bleiben?

Section Six — Free-time Activities

Speaking Track 9 — Photo card — p.32

Intro: Sag mir etwas über die Fotos.
1a) Was hast du in letzter Zeit im Fernsehen gesehen?
1b) Möchtest du auf ein Konzert gehen? Warum? / Warum nicht?
1c) Welche Art von Musik hörst du gern?
1d) Gehst du gern ins Kino? Warum? / Warum nicht?

Section Seven — Customs, Festivals and Celebrations

Speaking Track 10 — Reading aloud — p.36

Intro: Lies mir den Text vor.
2a) Wie möchtest du deinen nächsten Geburtstag feiern?
2b) Was sind die positiven Aspekte von Festen?
2c) Mit wem verbringst du gern Feste? Warum?
2d) Wie findest du Feuerwerke?

Section Eight — Celebrity Culture

Speaking Track 11 — Role-play — p.38

Intro: Du sprichst mit deinem Freund / deiner Freundin aus Österreich. Ich bin dein Freund / deine Freundin.
1) Was macht dein Lieblingsstar?
2) Wie sieht dein Lieblingsstar aus?
3) Warum magst du deinen Lieblingsstar?
4) Was denkst du über das Leben von Persönlichkeiten?
5) The student will now ask the teacher a question. The teacher should answer.

Theme 2 — Mixed Practice

Speaking Track 12 — Reading aloud — p.40

<u>Intro:</u> Lies mir den Text vor.

1a) Wie verbringst du gern deine Freizeit?

1b) Wie findest du Sport?

1c) Wie oft gehst du einkaufen?

1d) Was liest du gern?

Speaking Track 13 — Photo card — p.47

<u>Intro:</u> Sag mir etwas über die Fotos.

1a) Erzähl mir von Aktivitäten, die dich interessieren.

1b) Warum ist es wichtig, Freizeit zu haben?

1c) Sag mir etwas über deinen Lieblingssportstar.

1d) Möchtest du berühmt sein? Warum? / Warum nicht?

Section Nine — Travel and Tourism

Speaking Track 14 — Reading aloud — p.52

<u>Intro:</u> Lies mir den Text vor.

2a) Was isst du gern im Urlaub?

2b) Wie findest du Ferien auf dem Land?

2c) Gehst du gern im Urlaub einkaufen?
Warum? / Warum nicht?

2d) Wie entspannst du dich im Urlaub?

Section Ten — Media and Technology

Speaking Track 15 — Reading aloud — p.57

<u>Intro:</u> Lies mir den Text vor.

4a) Wie benutzt du soziale Medien in deinem Alltag?

4b) Was sind die Risiken von sozialen Netzwerken?

4c) Wem folgst du in den sozialen Medien?

4d) Sag mir etwas über eine App auf deinem Handy.

Section Eleven — Where People Live

Speaking Track 16 — Role-play — p.58

<u>Intro:</u> Du sprichst mit deinem Freund / deiner Freundin
aus Deutschland. Ich bin dein Freund / deine Freundin.

1) Sag mir etwas über einen typischen Morgen für dich.

2) Wann isst du normalerweise das Abendessen?

3) Wie findest du dein Haus?

4) Wie ist dein Schlafzimmer?

5) The student will now ask the teacher a question. The teacher
should answer.

Speaking Track 17 — Role-play — p.61

<u>Intro:</u> Du sprichst mit deinem Freund / deiner Freundin
aus der Schweiz. Ich bin dein Freund / deine Freundin.

1) Wie ist das Wetter in deiner Gegend?

2) Was machst du gern in deiner Gegend?

3) Was fehlt in deiner Gegend?

4) Würdest du lieber in einem Dorf oder in einer Stadt wohnen?
Warum?

5) The student will now ask the teacher a question. The teacher
should answer.

Section Twelve — Environmental and Social Issues

Speaking Track 18 — Photo card — p.62

<u>Intro:</u> Sag mir etwas über die Fotos.

2a) Was ist ein Umweltproblem, das dir Sorgen macht?

2b) Was hast du neulich für die Umwelt gemacht?

2c) Interessieren sich deine Freunde für die Umwelt?

2d) Was denkst du über grüne Energiequellen?

Speaking Track 19 — Role-play — p.65

<u>Intro:</u> Du sprichst mit deinem Freund / deiner Freundin
aus der Schweiz. Ich bin dein Freund / deine Freundin.

1) Beschreib mir eine Situation, in der du freiwillig gearbeitet hast.

2) Um welches soziale Problem sorgst du dich am meisten?

3) Wie kann die Regierung Menschen helfen, die Hilfe brauchen?

4) Wie würdest du anderen helfen?

5) The student will now ask the teacher a question. The teacher
should answer.

Theme 3 — Mixed Practice

Speaking Track 20 — Reading aloud — p.66

<u>Intro:</u> Lies mir den Text vor.

1a) Wie oft benutzt du das Internet?

1b) Was machst du auf deinem Handy?

1c) Was ist besser? Handy oder Laptop?

1d) Wie findest du das Einkaufen im Internet?

Speaking Track 21 — Photo card — p.73

<u>Intro:</u> Sag mir etwas über die Fotos.

1a) Welches Problem in der Welt macht dir am meisten Sorgen?
Warum?

1b) Was machst du persönlich, um die Umwelt zu schützen?

1c) Wie kann man anderen Menschen in der Gegend helfen?

1d) Glaubst du, dass soziale Medien gefährlich sind?
Warum? / Warum nicht?